"I like your Christ, I do not like your Christians. Your Christians are so unlike your Christ."

—Attr. Mahatma Gandhi

"The best evidence of Christianity is a Christ-like life, and the best evidence of the inspiration of the Word of God is found in the Word itself: when studied, loved, obeyed, and trusted, it never disappoints, never misleads, never fails."

—James Hudson Taylor

Copyright

The right of Duncan Matheson to be identified as the author of this work has been asserted to him under the Copyright and Design Patents Act 1988.

ISBN: 978-1-9164405-0-0 (paperback version).

ISBN: 978-1-9164405-3-1 (eBook version).

First published April 2019.

All rights reserved. Without limiting the rights under the copyright reserved above, no part of this publication may be reproduced, stored in or introduced into a retrieval system, or transmitted in any form or by any means (electronic, mechanical, photocopying, recording, or otherwise) without prior written permission.

For permission requests, please contact:

teachthemtoobey@gmail.com

Published by TTTO Ltd, Surrey, UK.

Scripture References

Unless otherwise noted, all Scripture quotations are taken from the HCSB®, Copyright © 1999, 2000, 2002, 2003, 2009 by Holman Bible Publishers. Used by permission. HCSB® is a federally registered trademark of Holman Bible Publishers.[1]

Scripture quotations marked (NIV) are taken from the Holy Bible, New International Version®, NIV®. Copyright © 1973, 1978, 1984, 2011 by Biblica, Inc.™ Used by permission of Zondervan. All rights reserved worldwide. www.zondervan.com. "NIV", and "New International Version" are trademarks registered in the United States Patent and Trademark Office by Biblica, Inc.™

Definitions

Unless otherwise stated, all selected definitions used are taken from the online Merriam Webster dictionary at http://www.merriam-webster.com.

Annotations and Footnotes

Any square brackets contained within Scripture references are those of the author to provide clarification or amplification where considered necessary.

Footnotes cited in this material do not imply any endorsement or approval of any website or other external materials by the author. The veracity of the articles has not been determined, and they are presented "as is" at the time of preparing this document. There is no guarantee that these links will continue to be valid.

Cover Design and Other Images

All images are sourced from Pixabay.com and edited by the author.

Editorial Development

The *Christian Writer's Manual of Style* by Robert Hudson has been used in the editorial development of this book.

---

[1] Please note that the HCSB uses capitalised pronouns for references to God, Jesus and the Holy Spirit (e.g. Him, His, and He, etc.) unlike most other Bible versions.

Reader Interactions

You can interact with Duncan Matheson at the following links:

Twitter: @teachthemtoobey

Facebook: https://www.facebook.com/teachthemtoobey.uk/

Website: www.teachthemtoobey.co.uk and www.teachthemtoobey.uk

Reviewer Comments

"The last verses of Matthew's Gospel have been called the Great Commission. Many have emphasised the challenge to 'go' even though it is not actually a command in the text. Some have rightly seen the call to make disciples as the principal command but have not gone on to discuss the method set out for that discipleship making – teaching people to obey the commands of Jesus and incorporating them into a new community through baptism. Duncan's book goes some way to filling that gap.

Duncan has applied his professional expertise to look systematically at the commands of Jesus as recorded in the Gospels. He classifies them as three expanding categories of Kingdom Fundamentals, Kingdom Practices, and Kingdom Behaviours.

For a serious follower of Jesus, these books could prove a very useful guide for a pattern of self-examination. Church groups would benefit from studying the books together and helping one another in the path of discipleship. It would be great if as a result of Duncan's books many more Christians exhibited the reality of Christlike living so that others might be drawn to become Jesus's disciples."

— Ray Porter – Chair of Global Connections and OMF International (UK).

As a minister and a missionary, I have studied the Great Commission in Matthew 28 dozens of times, and I have desired to align my life with Jesus's last command. Not long ago, the significance of his words, *"teach them to obey everything I have commanded you"*, pierced my heart. For years, I glossed over the word *obey,* perhaps because I preferred to think of the task as merely listing the commands of Christ. Teaching to obey is another thing entirely. It requires my own obedience as I make disciples. Duncan Matheson's work in this book is vital for any Christian. He categorizes more than eighty of Jesus's commands into three Kingdom Fundamentals and nine Kingdom Practices. This isn't a watering down of the Scriptures; it is a simplification for the purpose of practical obedience. The fourteen study sessions in the accompanying Studies for Disciples book allow us to follow Christ more closely by helping us understand the commands and work obedience into our lives. Highly recommended.

—Rev. Craig McClurg – Youth With A Mission (YWAM), USA.

"I think this is an eminently worthwhile project, and you have done an amazing job in bringing this material together in a way that would benefit any congregation. There is always a need for different kinds of good studies everywhere, especially those like yours that take a slightly different approach."

—Dr. David Harley – Former General Director of OMF International and former Principal at All Nations Christian College, England.

"Seeing more than eighty commands of Jesus all presented in such an approachable and structured way has gripped us right from the first chapter. As we turned the pages, we felt a combination of awed fascination alongside a deep challenge to our spirits as we were lovingly confronted with all the ways our Saviour has commanded us to live and grow.

It is impossible to have all of these scriptures march across your heart and not be profoundly affected by them. It was not hard to imagine Jesus speaking them to us directly as he would have done with his disciples.

Duncan has laid a challenge squarely before us in producing this work. Are we willing to obey what Jesus has commanded with no ifs and no buts?

We are already considering how we might share this experience with others as we come to grips with what Duncan has so clearly drawn together in his books. We commend them highly for all those who are serious about their walk of discipleship. To read them will leave you changed."

—Mark & Sue Vening – Trustees of YWAM Cymru/Wales.

"Duncan Matheson has strategically and accurately composed a wonderful resource for pastors, churches, and new believers that is bound to strengthen and encourage all in their journeys with Jesus. The use of charts and study questions draws the reader into a deeper contemplation of their role in radical obedience and practical ways to respond. Teach Them to Obey is truly a gift to Christians to help unlock a life of blessing and effectiveness as witnesses unto Christ."

—Ryan Peters – Director of Donor Management - Christ for All Nations - Canada.

"If Christians are serious about following the commands of Jesus in their own lives, this book offers a very helpful tool for personal discipleship and growth. It encourages readers to think about over eighty specific commands from Jesus in Scripture summarised into twelve themes. It also prompts readers to reflect on how they can practically work these out in their relationship with God, how they themselves can grow spiritually, and how they relate to others."

—Trevor Warner – Assistant Director for Mobilisation OMF UK.

"Jesus makes it clear that the wise person is the one who both hears his words and practices them. In this way our lives are built on a sure foundation. The Holy Spirit empowers us to follow Christ, but we also have a part to play in learning Jesus's commands as well as to obey them. Teach Them To Obey provides resources to do just that along with a systematic way in which the commands of Christ can be understood, remembered, and learned by practicing them together. I recommend this study to small groups who believe that Jesus truly has all authority and who desire to follow him and make disciples. As we connect Jesus's commands with the narrative of Scripture and the stories of our own lives, we can become attuned to cooperating with the Holy Spirit and bear much fruit to glorify our Father."

—John Peachey - YWAM missionary for thirty-five years, facilitator of the University of the Nations Masters in Christian Formation and Discipleship.

"John chapter 10 has been one of my favourite passages throughout my adult life. Jesus says that "the sheep recognise his voice and come to him." Duncan Matheson is undoubtedly one of his sheep, and *Teach Them to Obey* is the call to all Christians to lean into Jesus's commands, hear his voice afresh and come to him. As Jesus explains later in the passage, "I tell you the truth, I am the gate for the sheep . . . Those who come in through me will be saved. They will come and go freely and will find good pastures." If you are searching for a practical way to understand your role in finding good pastures, read these books."

—Mike Forsey, Assistant Executive Director, Salvation Army Community Services, Calgary, Alberta, Canada.

"I've now had a chance to review your books. You thoroughly challenged me as I did so, and I think that you've done an incredibly thorough job using Jesus's teaching to distil your hierarchy of behaviours, key attributes, and central idea."

—Murray Johnstone – Former Global Head of Succession and Development at PA Consulting Group, London.

"Your books are covering a topic that is very valuable in helping a Christian believer understand how Jesus taught his disciples by example and expected them to apply what they were being taught. I am supportive of the breakdown analysis, the actual spiritual content, and the overall focus of the books."

—Pastor Glyn Thomas – Frimley Baptist Church, Surrey, England.

"Most would agree that we have been commanded to make disciples, teaching them to obey the commands of Jesus (Matthew 28:19-20). Duncan has grouped these commands in a novel way to make them easier to remember and has developed a useful diagram to explain how they all fit together. He also suggests how we might put the commands into practice, helpfully relating his own experiences. This book will be of maximum benefit if used in a group study. I believe that all those who put this teaching into practice will find it transforms their lives for the better. It will also enable them to be a great help to others."

—Rev. Mike Johnson MA MMin – Retired Assemblies of God minister and Bible School tutor, Surrey, England.

"Teach Them to Obey is a rich menu that excites the palate. Jesus reveals the heart and mind of God the Father. Rigorous and thorough. A helpful structure of kingdom fundamentals, practices, and behaviours. Challenging!! Let us be salt and light in this world".

—David Leeper – Christian mentor and Founder of Let Hope Arise International, Africa.

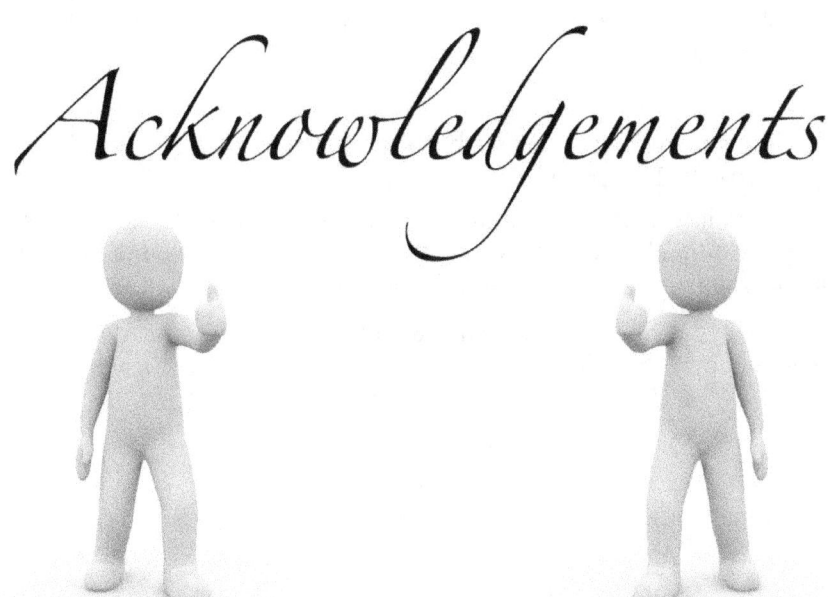

Acknowledgements

I would like to thank the following friends and colleagues for their thoughts and contributions on different sections or drafts of these books: Trevor Warner, Mark Vening, Rev. Mike Johnson, Allen McClymont, Rev. Ray Porter, Rev. Glyn Thomas, Dr Peter Rowan, Andy Smith, Murray Johnstone, my sister Maggie Matheson, my son Stuart, and daughter in law Amy Matheson. Many thanks too to Michele Hackney for her editorial support during the early drafting of these materials and subsequent careful proofreading. In particular I'd like to express my heartfelt gratitude to Jeanette Windle[2] for her diligent copy editing of these materials, her independent perspectives, and her advice concerning the publication process.

I would also like to thank the fellow followers of Jesus in my house group (Chris and Dawn, Mary, Kath, Sue, Andy, Frances, and Mary-Anne) for their perseverance and feedback as we worked through the *Studies for Disciples* materials and for their friendship in Christ over many years. I also wish to thank my wife Mary-Anne for her support during the development of these books and our many years together leading up to it.

---

[2] http://jeanettewindle.com/editing-services/

Pulling this all together, I am reminded of two scriptures:

> As iron sharpens iron, so one person sharpens another. (Proverbs 27:17, NIV)

and

> Plans fail for lack of counsel, but with many advisers they succeed. (Proverbs 15:22, NIV)

I have certainly benefited from the feedback of others, both personally and in regard to the development of the text, as I have attempted to make this material robust, defendable, readable, and theologically sound.

I hope that you enjoy this material and that it will become a blessing to you in your ongoing discipleship.

Preface

One of Jesus's final instructions to his disciples was that they should "teach them [other disciples] to obey everything that I have commanded you" (Matthew 28:20). However, his commands are peppered throughout the first five books of the New Testament and the early part of Revelation, so it is not easy to draw out the key themes of his teaching without some detailed analysis.

These Bible study books are the result of a comprehensive analysis of Scripture to identify Jesus's specific commands.[3] The material has been organised into a structural outline that can be readily comprehended and committed to memory by today's believers. In excess of eighty of Jesus's commands can be identified in the New Testament, each of which is presented in Figure 20.

The result of this analysis has been to group all of the scriptures from Jesus's commands into three top-level Kingdom Fundamentals. These are in turn supported by nine summary Kingdom Practices and a broader set of lower-

---

[3] It should be noted that where various Bible translations highlight Jesus's spoken words, they provide text that is an interpretation/approximation to what he said as he spoke in Aramaic, the New Testament was written in Greek, and it has been translated subsequently into English and other languages.

level Kingdom Behaviours (comprising either single or strongly related commands). All together, these encompass the two "greatest commandments" and the "Great Commission" (please see note on terminology below). The aim has been to describe these Kingdom Fundamentals and Kingdom Practices in an easily understood manner suitable for study by individuals, couples, or groups.

The analysis is supported throughout by comprehensive references to the words of Jesus directly from the New Testament. In many senses, the words of Jesus alone should be enough as the many available translations of Scripture (in English at least) make his instructions and commands quite clear.

Innumerable books have been written to help address the challenges of the Christian life. In this book, however, the objective has been to focus wholly on those things Jesus commanded his followers (i.e., Christians) to put into practice. Jesus's other teachings and wider instructions for godly living from the Old and New Testaments are not covered, although relevant references are provided where appropriate.

No claim is made here that those scriptures containing Jesus's commands are more important than any other scriptures within the Bible. The Christian life encompasses more than these. However, if we were to implement his commands alone, we could not go far wrong in our walk as his disciples.

As author of this analysis, I am keenly aware of my own deficiencies and failings in terms of the effective practice of all the things Jesus seeks from his disciples. We all have to rest in his marvellous grace, recognising that we are all "under construction", relying upon the Holy Spirit, Scripture, trusted fellow believers, and sound biblical teaching to help us move forward in our practical discipleship.

Intended Readership

This material is for anyone, whether they are new or established believers, who wants to understand what Jesus commanded his disciples to do and how to apply his teachings to their own lives. This distillation of Jesus's teaching may also have applications in an outreach or missions' context to help others begin to understand what being a follower of Jesus means.

Terminology and Outline Structure

Within this book, three terms have been adopted instead of using the words "Commandment" and "Discipline" in an effort to avoid reader confusion. Those words tend to have very specific or traditional meanings in Christian circles. The three terms used are:

> Kingdom Fundamentals—used to describe the three most important elements that summarise and develop the book's central theme, "Teach them to obey all that I have commanded you."

Kingdom Practices—used to define the key summarising themes that correspond to each Kingdom Fundamental.

Kingdom Behaviours—used to denote the various commands of Jesus that generally correspond to each Kingdom Practice and two of the Kingdom Fundamentals.

Figure 1 illustrates this pictorially in four levels, beginning with the theme of this book and moving through each fundamental and its supporting practices and behaviours.

In addition, when using the term "God", this book generally refers to the Trinity as a whole rather than God the Father. The Father, Son (Jesus), and Holy Spirit are separately identified where considered appropriate.

Figure 1 - Terminology and Structure Used in This Book

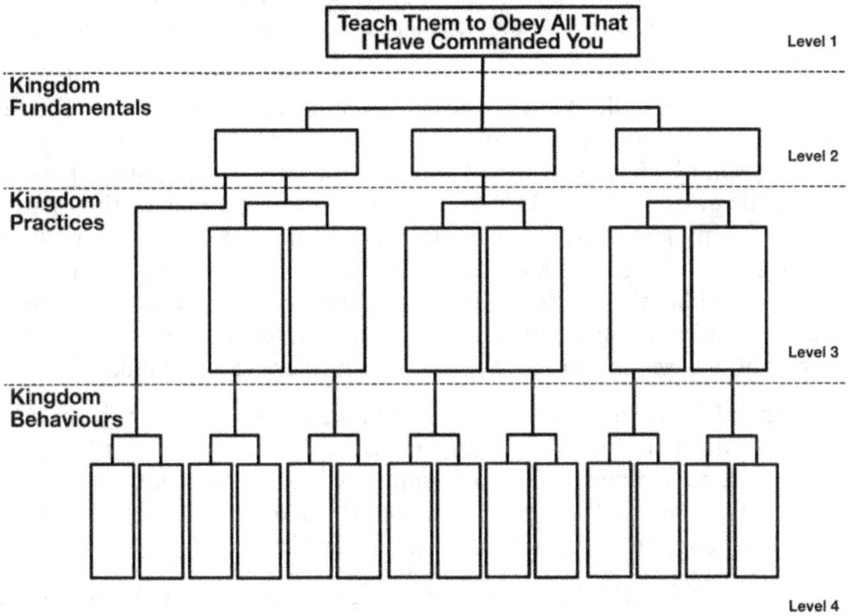

A Note on the Approach Underpinning This Book

In this book, the collated findings from a detailed analysis of Jesus's commands have been presented using a "top-down approach" based upon the method developed by Barbara Minto.[4] The book is targeted mainly at

---

[4] The Pyramid Principle. Barbara Minto, 2009, FT Prentice Hall (Pearson Education)

readers who are in Christian leadership as a source of reference as they seek to disciple others. It lays out all of Jesus's commands to his disciples, grouping and categorising them into a simple structure for followers to memorise and subsequently put into practice.

The story behind this Bible study material begins late in 2014 when I was reading the familiar words of Jesus in Matthew 28:19-20. His instruction to "teach them to obey all that I have commanded you" forced me to ask myself:

- What really did Jesus command his disciples to do?
- What were the main themes of Jesus's directive teaching?
- Has such an analysis already been done?
- Could Jesus's commands be analysed, grouped, and structured in such a way that would be relatively simple for me and others to remember?

I discovered that while studies of Jesus's commands had been done, I could find no such complete analysis as I envisioned. So I began my own investigation by identifying all the New Testament passages that reference commands given by Jesus. I grouped together those commands that shared a strong common message, summarizing them under specific biblical directives I refer to as Kingdom Behaviours (see above). In total, I uncovered within the words of Jesus eighty-four separate commands (other studies identify around fifty such commands, depending on differing interpretations; see the end of Appendix 1 for references and links).

The method I used in correlating these findings recognises that the human mind has difficulty remembering long lists. The average person easily recalls three to five items under one summary heading, and at most a list of eight items. So more than eighty Kingdom Behaviours would be extremely difficult for anyone to memorise as a single flat list.

Conversely, if I wanted to group these eighty-four commands (Kingdom Behaviours) into easily memorised lists of eight items or less, I would need a minimum of ten summarising ideas, or themes, under which to organise these Kingdom Behaviours. Indeed a list of ten would itself need to be further refined as this is clearly more than eight.

Also, without further elaboration and explanation, the list of Kingdom Behaviours I had assembled would not in itself help believers to be more effective in their life and witness. Nor would it offer anything markedly different from lists of Jesus's commands previously developed by others.

The challenge then was to develop a set of higher-level directives (Kingdom Practices and Kingdom Fundamentals) that successively grouped and summarised the set of Kingdom Behaviours. Let me make clear here that I am not suggesting there is any single right answer or unique solution. My own process involved a great many iterations, both in terms of levels and descriptive titles, before arriving at the results presented here.

In categorizing the eighty-four individual commands I'd found, it became clear to me that from Jesus's own perspective the two greatest commandments were unequivocally to love God and to love your neighbour as yourself (Mark 12:29-31). So in developing a "top-down" structure, it was essential that these two commands had to feature to some degree in the final result, becoming what are described here as the first and third of three Kingdom Fundamentals, as they will be referenced from here on out.

After considerable further analysis, I was able to group and summarise the eighty-four identified Kingdom Behaviours broadly into nine Kingdom Practices (themes). My next task was to determine whether all or some of these Kingdom Practices would fit under either of the Kingdom Fundamentals to Love God and Love Your Neighbour as Yourself. This proved to be the case in part (See Chapters 2 and 4 respectively). But some of the Kingdom Practices did not fit logically under either of these commandments. This was because they did not relate to loving God or one's neighbour but to the individual believer, internally to the believer's heart, character, and attitude, and externally to the believer's behaviours and actions.

To cut a long story short, I spent some months wrestling alone as well as in discussion with others over the development of what is set out as the second of the three Kingdom Fundamentals. This I have defined as Follow Jesus. The term recognises Jesus's repeated call to his disciples and others to "follow me." From my perspective, this made Follow Jesus a logical choice, resulting in three Kingdom Fundamentals overall.

Jesus wants us to become like him in our life and witness on earth, and to do so we not only have to love God and others but be changed on the inside as well (with the Holy Spirit's help). As we will see when we reach that point of the material, four of the nine Kingdom Practices (themes) under which individual commands (Kingdom Behaviours) have been organised are grouped under this Kingdom Fundamental to Follow Jesus (Chapter 3). The other five are grouped under the other two Kingdom Fundamentals of Love God and Love Your Neighbour as Yourself.

In preparing this material, I have analysed the scriptural content as presented in English-language translations. I am not a theologian. Neither am I a scholar of Greek or Hebrew. My main objective has been to develop these materials in a manner that is easy to understand, so that when readers have completed the book, they not only will have committed to memory the three Kingdom Fundamentals and nine Kingdom Practices but will be putting each of Jesus's commands into practice in their daily walk and witness as well as teaching them to others.

Table of Contents

Reviewer Comments	v
Acknowledgements	ix
Preface	xi
Foreword	xix
Chapter 1 – An Introductory Overview	1
Chapter 2 - Love God (the Trinity) – (KF1)	9
Chapter 3 - Follow Jesus – (KF2)	21
Chapter 4 - Love Your Neighbour as Yourself - (KF3)	43
Chapter 5 - Analysis Reflections	55
Appendix 1 - Further Reading on Discipleship	61
Appendix 2 - Summary of the Biblical Analysis	63

Foreword

The Church. Next to Jesus himself, the Church is God's best idea for the good of this world. Communities of Christ-followers organizing around Jesus's teaching for the purpose of experiencing, expressing, and extending God's love into this world.

The Church. Next to Satan himself, the Church is the worst influence that ever happened to this world. No institution has done more damage to people's understanding of the God who is love and his Kingdom of peace than the Church.

Both of these sentiments are true. The Church is either the best or worst thing for the advance of the Good News of Jesus in our world. There is little in between. What makes the difference? The centrality and supremacy of Jesus. History bears this out. When the Church loses its central theme of following Jesus, of learning, loving, and living out his teachings, and of making more disciples (students of the way of Jesus), the Church falls in love with the power of God minus the humble, other-centred love of God. Then what we call the "kingdom of God" becomes really just another kingdom of this world, now backed by misguided religious zeal in the name of Jesus.

Simply admonishing Christians to read their Bibles is not enough. Again, history shows us that more Bible reading without the way and words of Jesus at the centre does nothing to decrease violence, hypocrisy, and judgmentalism. In the sixteenth century when Protestants split with the

Catholic Church, their cry of "Sola Scriptura" offered the Church a renewed hope to get back on track. But in reading the Bible without Jesus at the centre, too many Protestants used the Bible to justify violence against Catholics, Anabaptists and other Protestant groups with differing doctrines, Jews, supposed witches, or anyone else they deemed heretical. Putting the Bible in the centre of our spiritual lives is one step shy of what Jesus calls us to do. Rather than hold centre place in our lives, the Bible should operate more like John the Baptist, pointing to Jesus and crying out, "Behold!"

What the Church needs in this and every generation is a commitment to the Word of God in print that centres on the Word of God in Person. Let's be clear! Healthy Christians don't follow the Bible. They read the Bible, study the Bible, and immerse themselves in the Bible—so they can follow Jesus. There is a difference. Mature Christians believe in the authoritative, inerrant, infallible Word of God, and his name is Jesus!

To religious leaders who read the Bible, studied the Bible, memorized the Bible, and followed the Bible, Jesus said:

> And the Father who sent me has himself testified concerning me. You have never heard his voice nor seen his form, **nor does his word dwell in you**, for you do not believe the one he sent. You study the Scriptures diligently because you think that in them you have eternal life. These are the very Scriptures that testify about me, yet you refuse to come to me to have life. (John 5:37-40, emphasis mine)

Jesus says it is possible to know the Bible and not know the Word of God. It is possible to hold Scripture dear to our hearts and not have God's Word dwelling in us. Every Christian should sit up and take notice. We've got work to do.

This is why I am so excited about any book that helps realign the Christian church with Christ. So much is at stake! That is why I am grateful to Duncan Matheson for the work he has invested in this project, and I'm grateful to you, the reader, for the time and energy I trust you are about to invest. Nothing could be more important. I really believe that.

To be clear, a study of the four Gospels does not mean we are abandoning the rest of the Bible for the words in red. But it does mean that we are aware that really learning and living the words of Jesus will put the rest of the Bible in its proper context. Learn the teachings of Jesus, meditate on them, discuss them, apply them, and then go into the rest of Scripture with renewed vision and purpose. See how the Old Testament prepares the way for Jesus and how the rest of the New Testament reflects back on and discusses the application of the teachings of Jesus. In this way, the Bible will no longer be a painting we mount on the wall to look at, but a window we install in a wall to look through until we see the face of Jesus.

Something that Christians and non-Christians, believers, atheists, and everybody in between can all agree on is that this world would be a better place if Christians learned to be more Christ-like. Imagine a future where communities of Jesus-followers around the world are living simply, loving boldly, and are spreading the Good News of Jesus with inclusion, compassion, and gentleness. I want to be a part of that movement. I want to lean into that future. I hope you do too.

Peace.

Bruxy Cavey. Teaching Pastor, The Meeting House, Ontario, Canada.

Chapter 1 - An Introductory Overview
Situation
In the final verses of his Gospel, Matthew records what Jesus said to his disciples at the end of Jesus's ministry on earth:

> Then Jesus came to them and said, "All authority in heaven and on earth has been given to me. Therefore, go and make disciples of all nations, baptising them in the name of the Father and of the Son and of the Holy Spirit, and teaching them to obey everything I have commanded you. And surely I am with you always, to the very end of the age." (Matthew 28:18-20, NIV)

This text is known within Christianity as the Great Commission. James Hudson Taylor, founder of the China Inland Mission, is quoted as saying the following about it:

> The Great Commission is not an option to be considered; it is a command to be obeyed.

All who are Jesus's followers, in whatever context God has placed them, need to consider this as part of their life of witness.

This book contains a complete analysis of all Jesus's commands. But understanding exactly what Jesus commanded his disciples to do in such a way that can be readily remembered is not easy since Jesus gave his disciples in excess of eighty of them. One way to help us memorise his teaching is to summarise these commands into a smaller set of "themes".

Throughout this book, these themes are referred to as Kingdom Fundamentals and Kingdom Practices. They fall into two basic categories: specific commands from Jesus during his earthly ministry and teachings we can glean from what Jesus himself practised while on earth as well as his specific promises concerning the Holy Spirit.

As we study Jesus's commands, however, we must keep in mind that our salvation in Jesus is not based upon anything we do, either before or after we become his disciples. Our justification is by grace through faith in him alone. This is why the gospel is itself "Good News".

The price for our sins is paid by Jesus's sacrifice on the cross, his death, and subsequent resurrection by God the Father. If we repent of our sins and take him as our Saviour and Lord, we are given the assurance of everlasting life now. As a result, we should be motivated to undertake acts of service for him. However, our promise of eternal life is not conditional on how we "perform", as we read in Romans 8:1-2:

> Therefore, there is now no condemnation for those who are in Christ Jesus, because through Christ Jesus the law of the Spirit who gives life has set you free from the law of sin and death. (NIV)

On Judgement Day we will be rewarded on the basis of our actions as Jesus's disciples, whereas non-believers (those who have not accepted his free offer of salvation) will face judgement as God, who is sovereign, determines.

Complications

People may label themselves as Christian without a true understanding of what commands a genuine disciple of Jesus should be actively living out. Being a follower of Jesus is not only about trying to put these teachings into practice, but also about having a Christ-like heart and attitude. Wanting to implement Jesus's commands in our lives should be a response that flows naturally from our salvation. Likewise, striving for consistency between our inner perspectives and our outward actions, i.e., being authentic in terms of what we say and do.

To illustrate, there is a marked difference between the UK's 2011 census, in which 59.5% of the population (37.5 million) identified itself as Christian,[5] and actual church membership within the UK, which in 2010 stood at only 11.2% of the population (5.5 million).[6] Similarly, 2014 data from the Pew Research Centre indicates that in the United States 70.6% of the population

---

[5] https://www.ons.gov.uk/peoplepopulationandcommunity/culturalidentity/religion/articles/fullstorywhatdoesthecensustellusaboutreligionin2011/2013-05-16

[6] Church Statistics - https://faithsurvey.co.uk/download/csintro.pdf - Page 2

identified themselves as Christian,[7] while only 39% or fewer actually attended church on a weekly basis.[8,9] From this it is clear that many who identify themselves as Christian are only nominally so.[10]

The global church has not done the best job in discharging Jesus's "Great Commission" (Matthew 28:18-20):

- Yes, we have gone.
- Yes, we have made converts/Christians, and many have become Jesus's disciples.
- Yes, we have also baptised a huge number of them.
- But no, we have definitely not systematically taught them to obey all that Jesus commanded.

In fact, the inconsistency of Christians in fulfilling what Jesus wants in terms of our actions, behaviours, and attitudes is one barrier to non-believers coming to know Jesus. If we were more Christ-like, more people might come into God's kingdom through accepting Jesus as their personal Saviour.

That said, it is important to recognise that there are other reasons why people don't accept Jesus:

- Human beings are sinful and will resist the truth in Jesus because they don't want to face up to this.
- There is a spiritual battle going on, whether we realise this or not.

---

[7] http://www.pewforum.org/2015/05/12/americas-changing-religious-landscape/
[8] http://www.gallup.com/poll/166613/four-report-attending-church-last-week.aspx
[9] http://www.churchleaders.com/pastors/pastor-articles/139575-7-startling-facts-an-up-close-look-at-church-attendance-in-america.html
[10] The Lausanne Committee for World Evangelization (LCWE) defines a nominal Christian as "a person who has not responded in repentance and faith to Jesus Christ as his personal Saviour and Lord." The LCWE notes that such a one "may be a practising or non-practising church member. He may give intellectual assent to basic Christian doctrines and claim to be a Christian. He may be faithful in attending liturgical rites and worship services, and be an active member involved in church affairs."

Muslim perceptions of Christians, for instance, are often confused by their classification of Western society[11] in general as being "Christian". The reality is, of course, far from this as secularism and atheism continue to increase in Western nations, while societal behaviours follow general cultural norms rather than any outworking of Christianity. To Muslim observers, Western practices such as different moral standards, the eating of pork, and consumption of alcohol are in conflict with teachings in the Qur'an as well as the Old Testament. So, to them, Christianity is also seen to be in conflict since they interpret that behaviour as "Christian". It should be noted here that the Muslim religion is highly rules-based whereas the Christian life is one of a developing relationship with a God who transforms the believer.

Many other faiths, people groups (i.e., people with common language and customs that may cross what are today's national boundaries), cultures, and nation states also view Christianity negatively.[12] Some reasons for this are because they do not understand:

- The nature of salvation in Jesus.
- What the Christian life should encompass.
- What the Christian life means for the individual believer.
- How Jesus's disciples should live their lives in their community, whether at home or abroad.

That many Christians do not follow the teachings of Jesus as much as they should is where our collective witness falls down. In consequence, the term Christian has become devalued at the very least. Such poor witness by some believers may be one reason why Mahatma Gandhi is reported to have said, "I like your Christ, but I do not like your Christians. Your Christians are so unlike your Christ." Whether it was in truth Gandhi who said this or someone else is secondary. It is the relevance of the words themselves we need to consider.

Even if we are poor witnesses, it is important to understand that this does not affect our salvation in Jesus as we are saved through faith and not works:

> For it is by grace you have been saved, through faith –and this is not from yourselves, it is the gift of God –not by works, so that no one can boast. For we are God's handiwork, created in Christ Jesus to do

---

[11] For example: the European Economic Area, USA and Canada, Australia and New Zealand
[12] http://www.opendoorsuk.org/persecution/country_profiles.php

> good works, which God prepared in advance for us to do. (Ephesians 2:8-9, NIV)

Jesus tells us in Luke 6:41-42:

> Why do you look at the speck that is in your brother's eye, but do not notice the log that is in your own eye? Or how can you say to your brother, "Brother, let me take out the speck that is in your eye," when you yourself do not see the log that is in your own eye? You hypocrite, first take the log out of your own eye, and then you will see clearly to take out the speck that is in your brother's eye.

What Jesus is teaching here is that as followers of Jesus we need to put our own lives in some sort of order before looking at the lives of others. Of course we must also recognise we can never be perfect in this life. This is precisely why we need to understand what Jesus is teaching so we can apply it to our own lives. Only then can we begin to help other believers become better disciples too.

So how can we do this? By applying the original command we've been discussing: "Teach them to obey all that I [Jesus] have commanded you."

This call to action implies the question: what exactly did Jesus command us so that we can subsequently do as he directs and teach others to obey those commands? To imitate Jesus better, we have to first understand what he commanded. This in turn entails seeking out within Jesus's teachings what those commands are and putting them into practice. Once we have done this, we will see that the commands Jesus gives us in Scripture can be summarised in terms of three Kingdom Fundamentals.

The first Kingdom Fundamental is one of the two "greatest commandments" cited by Jesus in Mark 12:30: to love God [the Trinity - God the Father, God the Son (Jesus), and God the Holy Spirit] with all our hearts and souls and minds and strength.

The second Kingdom Fundamental is Jesus's call to "follow me" (Matthew 4:19). In other words, we are to emulate Jesus, assisted by the Holy Spirit. Indeed, it is in recognition of this that we call ourselves followers of Jesus. Obeying this command is necessary before we can begin to implement the Great Commission as described in Matthew 28:18-20. In particular, we must become more like Jesus so that we can teach others to become more like him too. We will use the term Follow Jesus rather than "follow me" for this Kingdom Fundamental throughout the rest of this book.

The third Kingdom Fundamental is the second of the two commandments Jesus identifies as "greatest", which is to love your neighbour as yourself (Mark12:31). In other words, do to others as you would have them do to you (Luke 6:31).

We need to clarify that Jesus's command to love your neighbour as yourself is not a command to love yourself. On the contrary, the grammatical assumption in the text is that we already love ourselves, i.e., we put our own needs and wants naturally above those of others. This doesn't mean we shouldn't be comfortable with who we are. But Jesus's words here are much more about the need to live righteously, as we will discuss later.

If we look carefully, we can see that the two "greatest" commandments, to love God and to love our neighbour, are both outward-focused, from us towards God and towards others. In contrast, the second Kingdom Fundamental, which is for us to follow Jesus, focuses upon us as individuals. Following Jesus is the most important thing we can do if we are to allow him to rule and reign within us.

God through the Holy Spirit wants to develop and mould us into the people he created us to be. We need to be informed by Jesus's teaching and allow it to alter our internal attitudes and motivations, then our external actions, i.e., putting it into practice. If our lives reflect all Jesus commanded, our impact on a wider society will be more marked, drawing others to him as we demonstrate how loving God and God loving us can transform our lives and those with whom we come into contact.

That said, we must also recognise the warning Jesus gives in Mark 13:13:

> Everyone will hate you because of me, but the one who stands firm to the end will be saved. (NIV)

The observation attributed to Mahatma Gandhi accurately highlights the difference between the character of Jesus as recorded in the New Testament and the witness of too many who identify themselves as being his disciples. It does not take too much searching on social media or on the internet to see how even Christian-themed accounts and websites can present a less than wholesome view of Christianity, certainly one that Jesus would not recognise.

As followers of Jesus, we are called to be salt and light in the world, and within the confines of freedom of speech provisions, we should be prepared to express our views on matters of the day. However, these should be presented in a constructive, non-judgemental manner. We are not responsible for others' reactions to these views, whether defamatory, blasphemous, or otherwise. But we are responsible for how we subsequently interact, if at all. This is not saying that there is only one Christian viewpoint. Clearly, there are many varying perspectives on secular and faith matters. However, we should seek to be Christ-like in our dealings with others, not through ridicule or intolerance of others' views.

If we are to live as Jesus commands, then it follows that we need to understand what he requires of us. James Hudson Taylor, founder of the China Inland Mission, wrote:

> The best evidence of Christianity is a Christ-like life, and the best evidence of the inspiration of the Word of God is found in the Word

itself. When studied, loved, obeyed, and trusted, it never disappoints, never misleads, never fails.[13]

The Structure of This Book

The material set out in the next three chapters presents the full results of the analysis of all Jesus's commands to his disciples, grouped under the overarching message to "teach them to obey all that I have commanded you." This message is underpinned by the three Kingdom Fundamentals, which in summary call for us to understand, practise, and then teach others to love God, follow Jesus, and love your neighbour as yourself.

Chapter 2 covers the content of the analysis related to the Kingdom Fundamental to Love God. Chapter 3 does the same for those scriptures related to the Kingdom Fundamental to Follow Jesus. Chapter 4 presents those teachings of Jesus that describe and support the Kingdom Fundamental to Love Your Neighbour as Yourself.

Within each of these chapters, a number of Kingdom Practices have been presented, nine in total. Each Kingdom Practice is itself supported by a number of associated Kingdom Behaviours that collectively represent all New Testament references to Jesus's commands in a structured form.

The summary of the analysis in this book can be seen in Figure 2.

In Chapter 5 there are some simple questions for the reader to consider. These will allow you to reflect on what has been presented. Consider taking the time to ponder these and even to challenge the material and structure presented here. What terminology would you have used if you were to do this analysis? Consider going back to each individual command. How might you assemble them into different groupings? Consider developing your own summary terms for them. Perhaps you can construct your own structure that may be an even better representation of the totality of Jesus's commands. The potential possibilities are endless.

For my own part, my overarching purpose has been to develop a structure that will allow every reader to understand what Jesus commands his disciples to do. This in turn can provide a framework for readers to live out Jesus's commands in their day-to-day interactions with God and others. It can also provide a basis for us to help and instruct other believers in Jesus so that they in turn can seek to obey his commands better.

---

[13] https://archive.org/stream/HudsonTaylorsChoiceSayings-BroughtByPeter-johnParisis/HudsonTaylorsChoiceSayings-NotCopyrighted_djvu.txt

Figure 2 - The Overall Structure of Kingdom Fundamentals and Kingdom Practices under This Book's Main Message

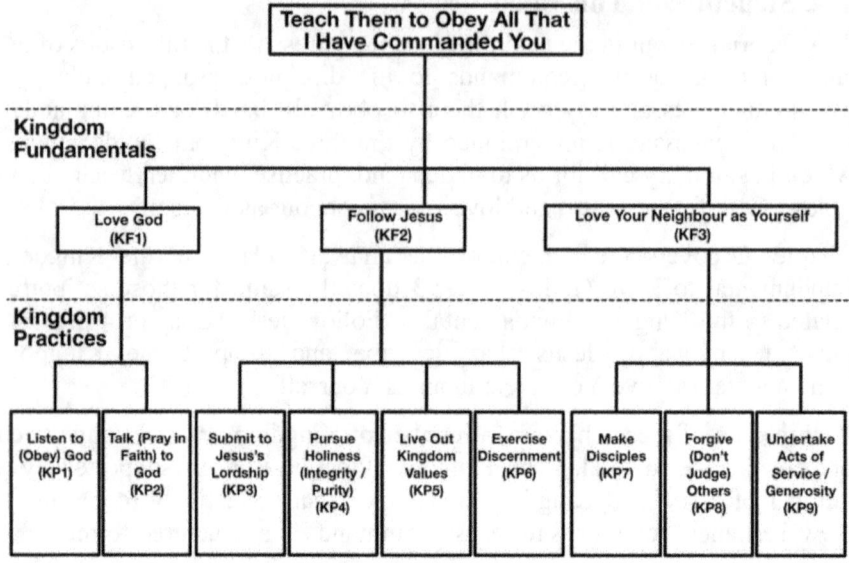

The analysis I have completed and am sharing with you here is undoubtedly not perfect. However, it does offer one approach to unlocking Scripture across different parts of the New Testament in a novel and unique way.

Chapter 2 - Love God (the Trinity) - (KF1)

As we saw in Chapter 1, among the last things Jesus is recorded as saying to his disciples, his final command to us as his followers, is that they, and we in turn, need to "teach them [other disciples] to obey everything that I [Jesus] have commanded you [his listeners]." We also saw that an analysis of Jesus's commands leads us to three Kingdom Fundamentals that are essential to our lives as Christians: to Love God, to Follow Jesus, and to Love Your Neighbour as Yourself.

In this chapter we will look at the teachings of Jesus that relate to the Kingdom Fundamental to Love God (see Figure 2). This is the first Kingdom Fundamental under the instruction from Jesus to "teach them all that I have commanded you."

When questioned by one of the Jewish legal specialists about what was most important, Jesus replied that the most important commandment is to love God. Scriptures that underpin this are:

> Love the Lord your God with all your heart, with all your soul, with all your mind, and with all your strength. (Mark 12:30; See also Matthew 22:37-38, Deuteronomy 6:5)

Interestingly, Jesus adds the term "all your mind" in his statement in Mark 30 when compared with Deuteronomy 6:5. In reply, we see that the teacher of the law and Jesus seem to agree that understanding God encompasses both soul and mind, leaving the heart perhaps as an emotional response and strength as our will or sheer determination. Verse 34 tells us that Jesus recognises that the man has answered wisely:

> "Well said, teacher," the man replied. "You are right in saying that God is one and there is no other but him. To love him with all your heart, with all your understanding and with all your strength, and to love your neighbour as yourself is more important than all burnt offerings and sacrifices." When Jesus saw that he had answered wisely, he said to him, "You are not far from the kingdom of God." And from then on no one dared ask him any more questions (Mark12:32-35, NIV).

In the two subsections that follow, teachings of Jesus that give some clarity as to how we are to love God have been organised under two supporting Kingdom Practices entitled:

- Listen to (Obey) God.
- Talk (Pray in Faith) to God.

These in turn are supported by a number of additional scriptures that are the actual words of Jesus. They have been grouped into a collection of Kingdom Behaviours as shown in Figure 3 and presented in Sections 2.1 and 2.2.

Figure 3 - Kingdom Fundamental 1 - to Love God - along with Supporting Kingdom Practices and Kingdom Behaviours

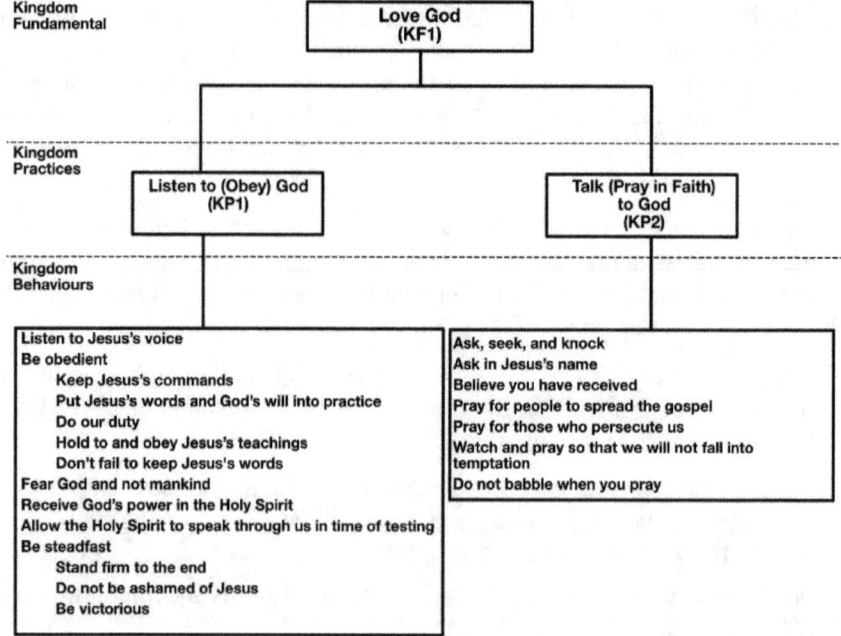

We have considered in the structural form shown in Figure 2 what the "most significant" messages are from Jesus's teaching. As we move forward, we will be using a set of diagrams that differs starkly from the more tiered, list-style outline structure presented in Figure 3. These diagrams will present how the set of Kingdom Fundamentals and Kingdom Practices can be considered *relationally* in terms of:

- First, our interactions (relationship) with God [the Trinity], i.e. Love God.
- Secondly, how these principles impact our own character (internal development/relationship); i.e., Follow Jesus.
- Lastly, how they influence our interactions (relationship) with others; i.e., Love Your Neighbour as Yourself.

The first example of this *relational perspective* can be seen in Figure 4, which focuses on our relationships with God and others as well as our own internal development as we seek to become more like Jesus.

Figure 4 - Followers Should Seek to Become More like Jesus as They Also Deepen Their Relationship with God and Others

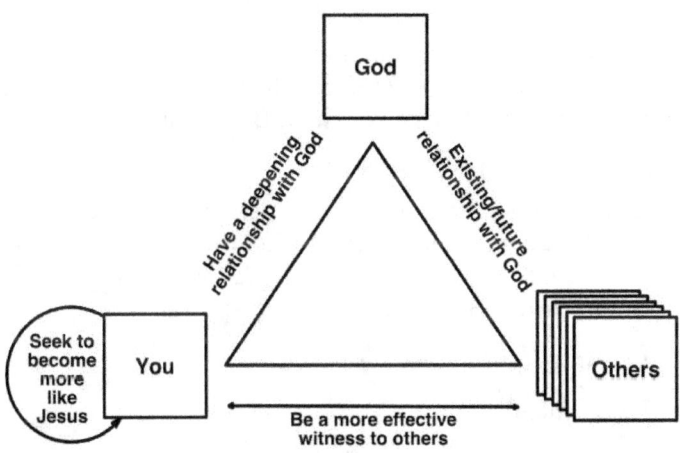

Our relationship with God at the highest level is illustrated in Figure 5. This relationship is supported by our understanding of God from the Bible and through the witness of the Holy Spirit.

Figure 5 - Kingdom Fundamental 1 - to Love God

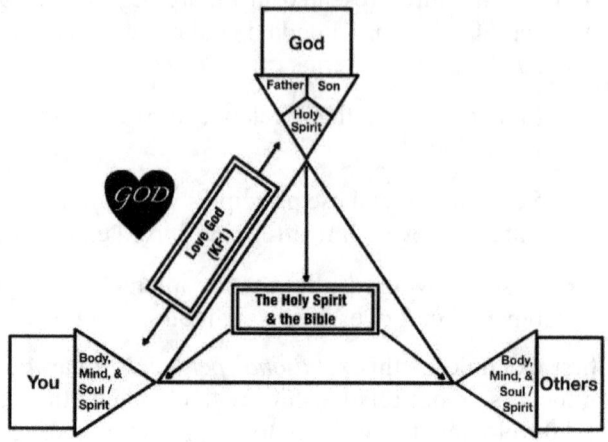

We will now look at two Kingdom Practices that correlate to the Kingdom Fundamental to Love God. Under each of these Kingdom Practices, we will consider a number of associated Kingdom Behaviours.

2.1 - Listen to (Obey) God - (KP1)

This subsection outlines the scriptures that define the first Kingdom Practice related to the Kingdom Fundamental to Love God, which is to Listen to (Obey) God. Jesus's commands that correlate to this practice have been grouped into six distinct Kingdom Behaviours:

- Listen to Jesus's voice.
- Be obedient.
- Fear God and not mankind.
- Receive God's power in the Holy Spirit.
- Allow the Holy Spirit to speak through us in time of testing.
- Be steadfast.

These are presented in subsections 2.1.1 to 2.1.6.

The relationship perspective is shown in Figure 6.

Figure 6 - Kingdom Practice 1 - to Listen to (Obey) God

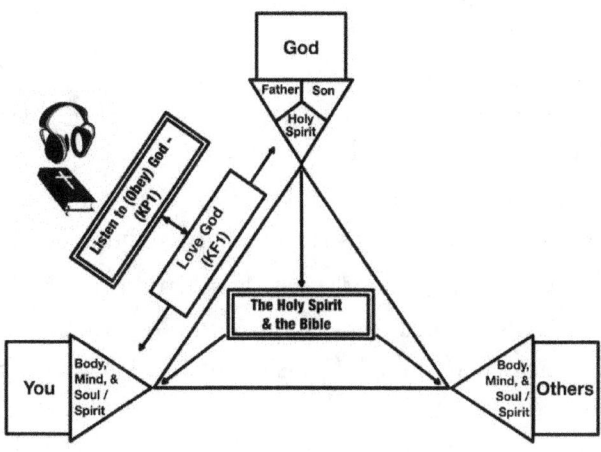

2.1.1 - Listen to Jesus's Voice

On a number of occasions, Jesus states that people need to listen to what he is saying. More than once, he warned those who had ears to listen.

> Anyone who has ears should listen. (Matthew 11:15)
>
> If anyone has ears to hear, he should listen. (Mark 4:23. See also, Matthew 13:43, Mark 4:9)

Scripture also records Jesus giving the same admonition after a parable or analogy.

> Still other seed fell on good ground; when it sprang up, it produced a crop: 100 times what was sown." As He said this, He called out, "Anyone who has ears to hear should listen!" (Luke 8:8)
>
> Now, salt is good, but if salt should lose its taste, how will it be made salty? It isn't fit for the soil or for the manure pile; they throw it out. Anyone who has ears to hear should listen. (Luke 14:34-35)

When Jesus sent out his own followers into ministry, he made clear that they were speaking on his behalf, so those who listened to their words were listening to Jesus.

> Whoever listens to you listens to Me. Whoever rejects you rejects Me. And whoever rejects Me rejects the One who sent Me. (Luke 10:16)

2.1.2 - Be Obedient

Jesus repeatedly states that we need to obey his teachings, which draw upon the following supporting Kingdom Behaviours:

Keep Jesus's Commands

The commands of Jesus are summarised throughout this book:

> If you love Me, you will keep My commands. (John 14:15)

Put Jesus's Words and God's Will into Practice

Our challenge as followers is to not only be hearers but doers too (James 1:22-25):

> Not everyone who says to Me, "Lord, Lord!" will enter the kingdom of heaven, but only the one who does the will of My Father in heaven. (Matthew 7:21)

> Therefore, everyone who hears these words of Mine and acts on them will be like a sensible man who built his house on the rock. The rain fell, the rivers rose, and the winds blew and pounded that house. Yet it didn't collapse, because its foundation was on the rock. (Matthew 7:24-25)

> Why do you call me, "Lord, Lord," and do not do what I say? As for everyone who comes to me and hears my words and puts them into practice, I will show you what they are like. They are like a man building a house, who dug down deep and laid the foundation on rock. When a flood came, the torrent struck that house but could not shake it, because it was well built. But the one who hears my words and does not put them into practice is like a man who built a house on the ground without a foundation. The moment the torrent struck that house, it collapsed and its destruction was complete. (Luke 6:46-49, NIV)

Do Our Duty

Even when we have done what Jesus asks, we have only discharged our responsibilities to him:

> Which one of you having a slave tending sheep or ploughing will say to him when he comes in from the field, "Come at once and sit down to eat"? Instead, will he not tell him, "Prepare something for me to eat, get ready, and serve me while I eat and drink; later you can eat and drink"? Does he thank that slave because he did what was commanded? In the same way, when you have done all that you

were commanded, you should say, "We are good-for-nothing slaves; we've only done our duty." (Luke 17:7-10)

Hold to and Obey Jesus's Teachings

By being obedient to Jesus, we will demonstrate our love for God and, through the Holy Spirit, will be liberated by the truth of God's Word:

> To the Jews who had believed him, Jesus said, "If you hold to my teaching, you are really my disciples. Then you will know the truth, and the truth will set you free." (John 8:31-32, NIV)

> Very truly I tell you, whoever obeys my word will never see death. (John 8:51, NIV)

> Jesus replied, "Anyone who loves me will obey my teaching. My Father will love them, and we will come to them and make our home with them. Anyone who does not love me will not obey my teaching. These words you hear are not my own; they belong to the Father who sent me." (John 14:23-24, NIV)

Don't Fail to Keep Jesus's Words

We have to respond to Jesus's teachings. If we reject them, then they will be the evidence against us:

> "If anyone hears my words but does not keep them, I do not judge that person. For I did not come to judge the world, but to save the world. There is a judge for the one who rejects me and does not accept my words; the very words I have spoken will condemn them at the last day." (John 12:47-48, NIV)

The sense here is that the text is directed at those who reject Jesus's message (non-Christians). However, might it also be considered as applying to those Christians who choose to ignore some of what Jesus is saying?

2.1.3 - Fear God Not Mankind

Jesus highlights that we need to fear God[14] and not people:

---

[14] The term "Fear God" is different from the concept of being terrified of something or someone. It is generally considered to include awe, adoration, respect for, and reverence towards God, although that is not immediately apparent in the quotations that are referenced.

> Don't fear those who kill the body but are not able to kill the soul; rather, fear Him who is able to destroy both soul and body in hell. (Matthew 10:28)
>
> And I say to you, My friends, don't fear those who kill the body, and after that can do nothing more. But I will show you the One to fear: Fear Him who has authority to throw people into hell after death. Yes, I say to you, this is the One to fear. (Luke 12:4-5)

2.1.4 - Receive God's Power in the Holy Spirit

Receive: To act as a receptacle or container for: to permit to enter.

Jesus promises that our lives as his followers will be empowered by the gift of the Holy Spirit:

> And look, I am sending you what My Father promised. As for you, stay in the city until you are empowered from on high. (Luke 24:49)
>
> But the Counsellor, the Holy Spirit –the Father will send Him in My name –will teach you all things and remind you of everything I have told you. (John 14:26)
>
> And with that he breathed on them and said, "Receive the Holy Spirit. If you forgive anyone's sins, their sins are forgiven; if you do not forgive them, they are not forgiven." (John 20:22-23, NIV)
>
> But you will receive power when the Holy Spirit has come on you, and you will be My witnesses in Jerusalem, in all Judea and Samaria, and to the ends of the earth. (Acts 1:8)

2.1.5 - Allow the Holy Spirit to Speak through Us in Time of Testing

When we face difficulties, Jesus reminds us that we should not worry what we are to say as the Holy Spirit will speak on our behalf:

> Whenever they bring you before synagogues and rulers and authorities, don't worry about how you should defend yourselves or what you should say. For the Holy Spirit will teach you at that very hour what must be said. (Luke 12:11-12. See also Matthew 10:19-20, Mark 13:11)

2.1.6 - Be Steadfast

Collectively, the following supporting Kingdom Behaviours can be summarised as the need to be steadfast:

Stand Firm to the End

We need to keep to Jesus's teachings in all circumstances:

> You will be hated by everyone because of me, but the one who stands firm to the end will be saved. When you are persecuted in one place, flee to another. Truly I tell you, you will not finish going

through the towns of Israel before the Son of Man comes. (Matthew 10:22-23, NIV. See also Matthew 24:13, Mark 13:13)

Do Not Be Ashamed of Jesus

Jesus requires us to be true to him, particularly among unbelievers:

> For whoever is ashamed of Me and of My words in this adulterous and sinful generation, the Son of Man will also be ashamed of him when He comes in the glory of His Father with the holy angels. (Mark 8:38. See also Luke 9:26, Luke 12:8-9)

Be Victorious

Jesus makes a series of promises for those who remain obedient to him:

> Anyone who has an ear should listen to what the Spirit says to the churches. I will give the victor the right to eat from the tree of life, which is in God's paradise. (Revelation 2:7)

> Anyone who has an ear should listen to what the Spirit says to the churches. The victor will never be harmed by the second death. (Revelation 2:11)

> Anyone who has an ear should listen to what the Spirit says to the churches. I will give the victor some of the hidden manna. I will also give him a white stone, and on the stone a new name is inscribed that no one knows except the one who receives it. (Revelation 2:17)

> The one who is victorious and keeps My works to the end: I will give him authority over the nations – and he will shepherd them with an iron sceptre; he will shatter them like pottery – just as I have received this from My Father. I will also give him the morning star. (Revelation 2:26-28)

> In the same way, the victor will be dressed in white clothes, and I will never erase his name from the book of life but will acknowledge his name before My Father and before His angels. (Revelation 3:5)

> The victor: I will make him a pillar in the sanctuary of My God, and he will never go out again. I will write on him the name of My God and the name of the city of My God – the new Jerusalem, which comes down out of heaven from My God – and My new name. (Revelation 3:12)

> The victor: I will give him the right to sit with Me on My throne, just as I also won the victory and sat down with My Father on His throne. (Revelation 3:21)

2.2 - Talk (Pray in Faith) to God - (KP2)

Here we are looking at the scriptures that underpin the Kingdom Practice to Talk (Pray in Faith) to God. This is the second Kingdom Practice that correlates to the Kingdom Fundamental to Love God. It is in turn supported by a number of related commands Jesus gave that have been grouped into seven distinct Kingdom Behaviours:

- Ask, seek, and knock.
- Ask in Jesus's name.
- Believe you have received.
- Pray for people to spread the gospel.
- Pray for those who persecute us.
- Watch and pray so that we will not fall into temptation.
- Do not babble when you pray.

These are presented in subsections 2.2.1 to 2.2.5.

The relationship perspective is shown in Figure 7.

Figure 7 - Kingdom Practice 2 - to Talk (Pray in Faith) to God

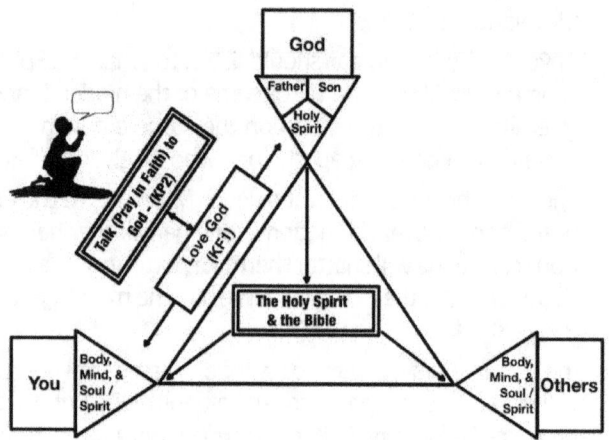

2.2.1 - Ask, Seek, and Knock

Jesus tells us to keep asking in prayer for the things that concern us:

> So I say to you: Ask and it will be given to you; seek and you will find; knock and the door will be opened to you. (Luke 11:9, NIV. See also Matthew 7:7-8)

2.2.2 - Ask in Jesus's Name

When we pray, we are to ask as in his name as we do not have any right to ask on our own behalf:

> I assure you: The one who believes in Me will also do the works that I do. And he will do even greater works than these, because I am going to the Father. Whatever you ask in My name, I will do it so that the Father may be glorified in the Son. If you ask Me anything in My name, I will do it (John 14:12-14).

2.2.3 - Believe You Have Received

Jesus states that we will be rewarded if we believe that God will answer when we pray:

> But when you pray, go into your room, close the door and pray to your Father, who is unseen. Then your Father, who sees what is done in secret, will reward you. (Matthew 6:6, NIV)

> Jesus answered them, "I assure you: If you have faith and do not doubt, you will not only do what was done to the fig tree, but even if you tell this mountain, 'Be lifted up and thrown into the sea,' it will be done. And if you believe, you will receive whatever you ask for in prayer." (Matthew 21:21-22)

> Therefore I tell you, all the things you pray and ask for –believe that you have received them, and you will have them. (Mark 11:24)

> If you remain in Me and My words remain in you, ask whatever you want and it will be done for you. (John 15:7)

2.2.4 - Pray for People to Spread the Gospel

Jesus highlights that we need to pray for more people to spread the gospel:

> He told them: "The harvest is abundant, but the workers are few. Therefore, pray to the Lord of the harvest to send out workers into His harvest." (Luke 10:2. See also Matthew 9:37-38)

2.2.5 - Pray for Those Who Persecute Us

This is a particular challenge from Jesus to pray positively for those who mistreat us:

> But I tell you, love your enemies and pray for those who persecute you. (Matthew 5:44)
>
> But I say to you who listen: Love your enemies, do what is good to those who hate you, bless those who curse you, pray for those who mistreat you. (Luke 6:27-28)

2.2.6 - Watch and Pray So We Will Not Fall into Temptation

Jesus commanded his disciples to be vigilant, especially in the face of worldly things around us:

> Stay awake and pray, so that you won't enter into temptation. The spirit is willing, but the flesh is weak. (Matthew 26:41)

2.2.7 - Do Not Babble When You Pray

Jesus tells us to be concise and to the point when we pray:

> And when you pray, do not keep on babbling like pagans, for they think they will be heard because of their many words. Do not be like them, for your Father knows what you need before you ask Him. (Matthew 6:7-8, NIV)

Chapter 3 - Follow Jesus - (KF2)

In the previous chapter we considered the Kingdom Fundamental to Love God and its two supporting Kingdom Practices. This next chapter presents the commands of Jesus that correlate to the Kingdom Fundamental to Follow Jesus (see Figure 2). This is the second element that has been grouped under the instruction from Jesus to "teach them all that I have commanded you."

We have already highlighted what Jesus considered the two greatest commandments for his disciples to follow (covered in Chapters 2 and 4). Along with these two, the most significant command Jesus gives, which if obeyed encompasses all other commands, is his call to "follow me." Time and time again during his ministry, Jesus issued this call to a wide variety of people, and indeed for almost two thousand years Christians have referred to themselves as being his followers (or disciples). A number of scriptures that centre around the call to follow Jesus and what it means can be grouped into six distinct Kingdom Behaviours. These are described more fully below and listed on the left-hand side of Figure 8.

- Respond to the call to follow.
- Don't make excuses.
- Know Jesus's voice.
- Follow and serve Jesus.

- Calculate the cost (deny yourself and take up your cross).
- Receive rest from Jesus.

Figure 8 - The Kingdom Practices and Kingdom Behaviours That Underpin the Kingdom Fundamental to Follow Jesus

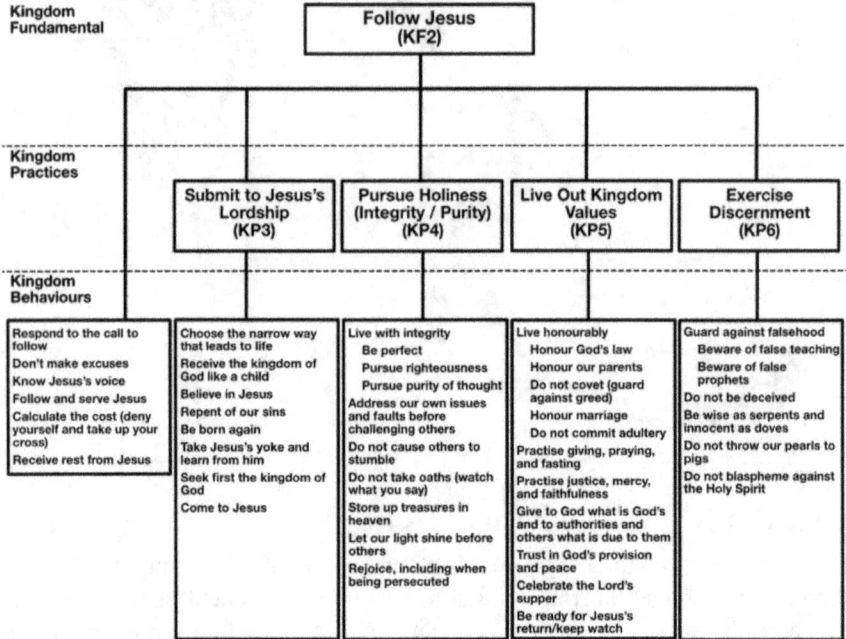

Respond to the Call to Follow

Jesus called specific people to "follow me." He calls us to do the same, so we need to decide how we will respond. You will notice below that not every reference to Jesus's call to "follow me" is worded strictly in the form of a command. But each still gives a clear sense of the importance Jesus attaches to wanting people to follow him:

"Follow Me," He told them, "and I will make you fish for people!" (Matthew 4:19. See also Mark 1:17)

Then, moving on, He saw Levi the son of Alphaeus sitting at the tax office, and He said to him, "Follow Me!" So he got up and followed Him. (Mark 2:14. See also Matthew 9:9, Luke 5:27)

The next day He decided to leave for Galilee. Jesus found Philip and told him, "Follow Me!" (John 1:43)

He said this to signify by what kind of death he would glorify God. After saying this, He told him, "Follow Me!" (John 21:19)

"If I want him to remain until I come," Jesus answered, "what is that to you? As for you, follow Me." (John 21:22)

Don't Make Excuses

If we are to respond to the call of Jesus, we must not delay in doing so:

As they were traveling on the road someone said to Him, "I will follow You wherever You go!" Jesus told him, "Foxes have dens, and birds of the sky have nests, but the Son of Man has no place to lay His head." Then He said to another, "Follow Me." "Lord," he said, "first let me go bury my father." But He told him, "Let the dead bury their own dead, but you go and spread the news of the kingdom of God." Another also said, "I will follow You, Lord, but first let me go and say good-bye to those at my house". But Jesus said to him, "No one who puts his hand to the plough and looks back is fit for the kingdom of God." (Luke 9:57-62. See also Matthew 8:18-22)

Know Jesus's Voice

As we grow in our knowledge of Jesus, we will become more familiar with his voice:

My sheep hear My voice, I know them, and they follow Me. I give them eternal life, and they will never perish – ever! No one will snatch them out of My hand. My Father, who has given them to Me, is greater than all. No one is able to snatch them out of the Father's hand. (John 10:27-29)

Follow and Serve Jesus

Just as Jesus came as a servant, we must adopt this role if we are to truly follow him:

If anyone serves Me, he must follow Me. Where I am, there My servant also will be. If anyone serves Me, the Father will honour him. (John 12:26)

Calculate the Cost (Deny Yourself and Take Up Your Cross)

We must consider the cost of being a disciple because Jesus does not promise that all our troubles will stop when we make a decision to follow him:

> And whoever doesn't take up his cross and follow Me is not worthy of Me. Anyone finding his life will lose it, and anyone losing his life because of Me will find it. (Matthew 10:38-39)
>
> Then Jesus said to His disciples, "If anyone wants to come with Me, he must deny himself, take up his cross, and follow Me. For whoever wants to save his life will lose it, but whoever loses his life because of Me will find it." (Matthew 16:24-25. See also Mark 8:34-35, Luke 9:23-24)
>
> Now great crowds were traveling with Him. So He turned and said to them: "If anyone comes to Me and does not hate his own father and mother, wife and children, brothers and sisters –yes, and even his own life –he cannot be My disciple. Whoever does not bear his own cross and come after Me cannot be My disciple. For which of you, wanting to build a tower, doesn't first sit down and calculate the cost to see if he has enough to complete it? Otherwise, after he has laid the foundation and cannot finish it, all the onlookers will begin to make fun of him, saying, "This man started to build and wasn't able to finish." Or what king, going to war against another king, will not first sit down and decide if he is able with 10,000 to oppose the one who comes against him with 20,000? If not, while the other is still far off, he sends a delegation and asks for terms of peace. In the same way, therefore, every one of you who does not say good-bye to all his possessions cannot be My disciple." (Luke 14:25-33)

Receive Rest from Jesus

Jesus offers people with troubles and challenges a specific invitation to come to him and receive the rest only he can give:

> Come to Me, all of you who are weary and burdened, and I will give you rest. All of you, take up My yoke and learn from Me, because I am gentle and humble in heart, and you will find rest for yourselves. For My yoke is easy and My burden is light. (Matthew 11:28-30)

Four Kingdom Practices have been identified that correlate to the Kingdom Fundamental to Follow Jesus:

- Submit to Jesus's Lordship.
- Pursue holiness (integrity/purity).
- Live out kingdom values.
- Exercise discernment.

Each of these Kingdom Practices is supported by various related Kingdom Behaviours as illustrated in Figure 8. Underpinning the Kingdom Behaviours are Jesus's own words as given in additional scriptures, which are detailed within subsections 3.1 to 3.4.

Figure 9 shows that the call and response to Follow Jesus is something personal to each of us and in many senses internal. Yes, we have to work out our faith with God and others in a practical sense. But following Jesus also involves God changing us internally through his Holy Spirit to become more like Jesus.

Figure 9 - Kingdom Fundamental 2 - to Follow Jesus

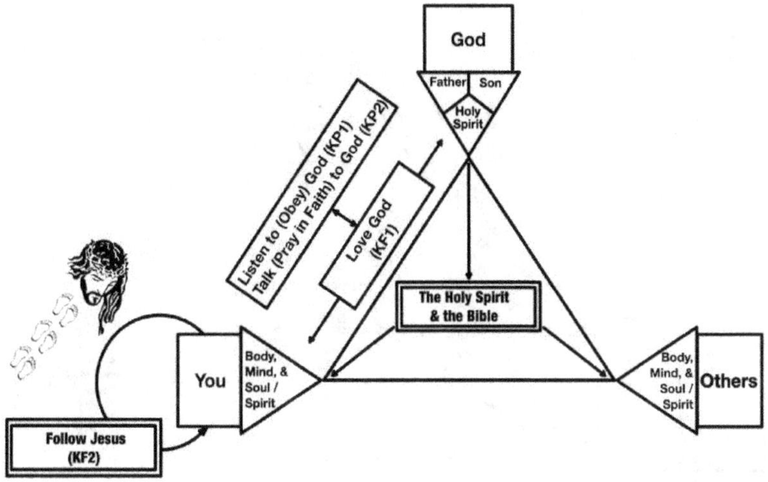

3.1 - Submit to Jesus's Lordship - (KP3)

In this subsection, we will be considering scriptures that give an overall description of the first Kingdom Practice underpinning the Kingdom Fundamental to Follow Jesus, which is to Submit to Jesus's Lordship. Commands of Jesus that support this Kingdom Practice have been grouped into eight distinct Kingdom Behaviours:

- Choose the narrow way that leads to life.
- Receive the kingdom of God like a child.
- Believe in Jesus.
- Repent of our sins.
- Be born again.
- Take Jesus's yoke and learn from him.
- Seek first the kingdom of God.

- Come to Jesus.

The scriptures that define each Kingdom Behaviour are presented in subsections 3.1.1 to 3.1.8 below.

The relationship perspective is shown in Figure 10.

Figure 10 - Kingdom Practice 3 - to Submit to Jesus's Lordship

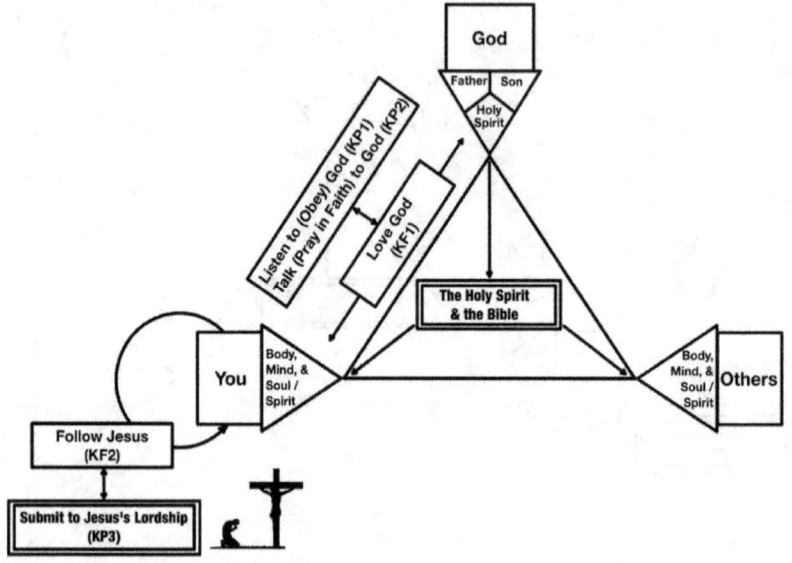

3.1.1 - Choose the Narrow Way That Leads to Life

Jesus tells us that he is the way, the truth, and the life and that the only way into the kingdom of God is through him:

> Jesus answered, "I am the way and the truth and the life. No one comes to the Father except through me." (John 14:6, NIV)
>
> Enter through the narrow gate. For the gate is wide and the road is broad that leads to destruction, and there are many who go through it. How narrow is the gate and difficult the road that leads to life, and few find it. (Matthew 7:13-14)
>
> Make every effort to enter through the narrow door, because I tell you, many will try to enter and won't be able once the homeowner gets up and shuts the door. Then you will stand outside and knock on the door, saying, "Lord, open up for us!" He will answer you, "I don't know you or where you're from." Then you will say, "We ate and drank in Your presence, and You taught in our streets!" But He will say, "I tell you, I don't know you or where you're from. Get away from Me, all you workers of unrighteousness!" There will be

weeping and gnashing of teeth in that place, when you see Abraham, Isaac, Jacob, and all the prophets in the kingdom of God but yourselves thrown out. They will come from east and west, from north and south, and recline at the table in the kingdom of God. Note this: Some are last who will be first, and some are first who will be last. (Luke 13:24-30)

3.1.2 - Receive the Kingdom of God like a Child

Jesus explains that we must be child-like (trusting simply) in our approach to coming into the kingdom. We cannot intellectualise it or approach it on our own terms:

> I assure you: Whoever does not welcome the kingdom of God like a little child will never enter it. (Mark 10:15. See also Luke 18:17)

3.1.3 - Believe in Jesus

Jesus encourages us to believe in him:

> Your heart must not be troubled. Believe in God; believe also in Me. (John 14:1)

> I assure you: Anyone who hears My word and believes Him who sent Me has eternal life and will not come under judgment but has passed from death to life. (John 5:24)

> Jesus replied, "This is the work of God –that you believe in the One He has sent." (John 6:29)

3.1.4 - Repent of Our Sins

We must repent if we are to receive the benefits of Jesus's sacrifice, including forgiveness for our sins and the promise of eternal life beginning now:

> From then on Jesus began to preach, "Repent, because the kingdom of heaven has come near." (Matthew 4:17)

> After John was arrested, Jesus went to Galilee, preaching the good news of God: "The time is fulfilled, and the kingdom of God has come near. Repent and believe in the good news." (Mark 1:14-15)

> No, I tell you; but unless you repent, you will all perish as well. (Luke 13:3. See also Luke 13:5)

3.1.5 - Be Born Again

Only by accepting Jesus as our Saviour can our spiritual life commence as we receive the Holy Spirit and begin a relationship with God and Jesus:

> Do not be amazed that I told you that you must be born again. (John 3:7)

3.1.6 - Take Jesus's Yoke and Learn from Him

When we come to Jesus and trust in him for all things, the challenges we have will be made more bearable, though this is not a promise that all challenges will go away:

> All of you, take up My yoke and learn from Me, because I am gentle and humble in heart, and you will find rest for yourselves. For My yoke is easy and My burden is light. (Matthew 11:29-30)

3.1.7 - Seek First the Kingdom of God

When we put the increase of God's kingdom ahead of everything else, God will then supply all our needs for life:

> But seek first the kingdom of God and His righteousness, and all these things will be provided for you. (Matthew 6:33)

> Consider how the wildflowers grow: They don't labour or spin thread. Yet I tell you, not even Solomon in all his splendour was adorned like one of these! If that's how God clothes the grass, which is in the field today and is thrown into the furnace tomorrow, how much more will He do for you –you of little faith? Don't keep striving for what you should eat and what you should drink, and don't be anxious. For the Gentile world eagerly seeks all these things, and your Father knows that you need them. But seek His kingdom, and these things will be provided for you. (Luke 12:27-31)

3.1.8 - Come to Jesus

When we choose to follow Jesus, we begin our spiritual life in him. We also receive the gift of the Holy Spirit, who as we allow him will help us to love God and show Jesus's love to others "from the inside out".

> On the last and most important day of the festival, Jesus stood up and cried out, "If anyone is thirsty, he should come to Me and drink! The one who believes in Me, as the Scripture has said, will have streams of living water flow from deep within him." He said this about the Spirit. Those who believed in Jesus were going to receive the Spirit, for the Spirit had not yet been received because Jesus had not yet been glorified. (John 7:37-39)

3.2 - Pursue Holiness (Integrity/Purity) - (KP4)

Here we consider the scriptures underpinning the second Kingdom Practice that correlates to the Kingdom Fundamental to Follow Jesus, which is to Pursue Holiness (Integrity/Purity). This Kingdom Practice is in turn supported by related commands of Jesus that have been grouped into seven distinct Kingdom Behaviours:

- Live with integrity.
- Address our own issues and faults before challenging others.
- Do not cause others to stumble.
- Do not take oaths (watch what you say).
- Store up treasures in heaven.
- Let our light shine before others.

- Rejoice, including when being persecuted.

The commands of Jesus relevant to each Kingdom Behaviour are presented in subsections 3.2.1 to 3.2.7.

The relationship perspective is shown in Figure 11.

Figure 11 - Kingdom Practice 4 - to Pursue Holiness (Integrity/Purity)

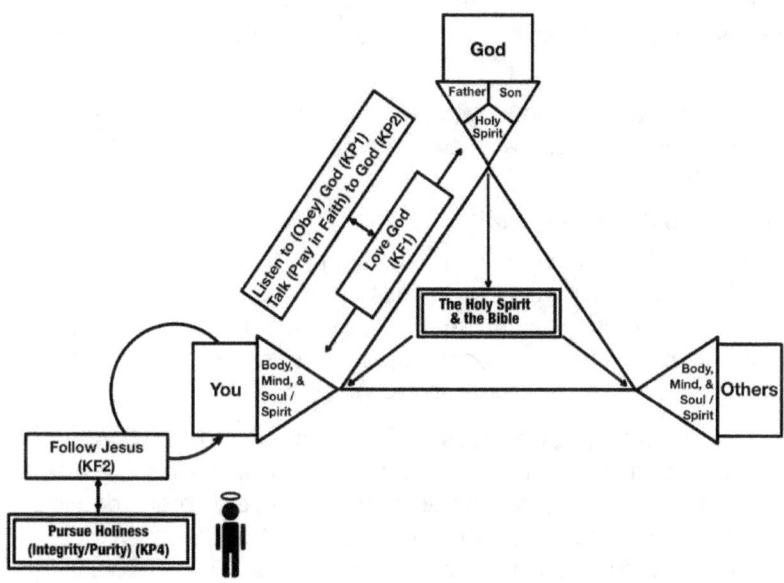

3.2.1 - Live with Integrity

As followers of Jesus, we are to be consistent in what we think and say and more importantly in what we do, including the supporting Kingdom Behaviours that follow:

Be Perfect

Jesus challenges us to be perfect. However, this does not necessarily mean perfect in the simplest understanding of the term (without fault or blemish), although it can be looked at that way. Other interpretations include the concept of completeness, maturity, consistency, and integrated. From these we can infer the need for integrity in terms of our thoughts and actions.

This command immediately follows his instruction to love our enemies. So one way in which Jesus is calling us here to be perfect may be in how we love others, including our enemies. As we seek to obey this command with the help of the Holy Spirit, we will need to remain humble and dependent upon him:

> Be perfect, therefore, as your heavenly Father is perfect. (Matthew 5:48)

Pursue Righteousness

Guided by the Holy Spirit, we should strive to be like Jesus in all our actions, whether we are alone or with others. His words below were said to the Jews to highlight that they were unable to live up to standards set by God. While they are not technically a command of Jesus to his followers, they highlight that earthly religious leaders should not be our standard for righteousness but Jesus himself:

> For I tell you, unless your righteousness surpasses that of the scribes and Pharisees, you will never enter the kingdom of heaven. (Matthew 5:20)

Pursue Purity of Thought

We must strive always to keep our thought life wholesome (see also the second part of 2 Corinthians 10:5). The reference below is again not strictly a command from Jesus, but Jesus is making clear the correlation between impurity of thought and sinful behaviour. (see also Matthew 5:27-28):

> Then He said, "What comes out of a person –that defiles him. For from within, out of people's hearts, come evil thoughts, sexual immoralities, thefts, murders, adulteries, greed, evil actions, deceit, promiscuity, stinginess, blasphemy, pride, and foolishness. All these evil things come from within and defile a person." (Mark 7:20-23).

3.2.2 - Address Our Own Issues and Faults before Challenging Others

Jesus requires us to examine and sort out our own hearts, behaviours, and attitudes before we consider rebuking or correcting a fellow brother or sister in God's family:

> Why do you look at the speck in your brother's eye, but don't notice the log in your own eye? Or how can you say to your brother, "Brother, let me take out the speck that is in your eye," when you yourself don't see the log in your eye? Hypocrite! First take the log out of your eye, and then you will see clearly to take out the speck in your brother's eye. (Luke 6:41-42. See also Matthew 7:3-5)

3.2.3 - Do Not Cause Others to Stumble

The way in which we act, whether in private or in public, should not be a basis for leading someone else to do anything of which God would not approve:

> But whoever causes the downfall of one of these little ones[15] who believe in Me – it would be better for him if a heavy millstone were hung around his neck and he were drowned in the depths of the sea! Woe to the world because of offences. For offences must come, but woe to that man by whom the offence comes. (Matthew 18:6-7)
>
> But whoever causes the downfall of one of these little ones who believe in Me – it would be better for him if a heavy millstone were hung around his neck and he were thrown into the sea. (Mark 9:42)
>
> He said to His disciples, "Offences will certainly come, but woe to the one they come through! It would be better for him if a millstone were hung around his neck and he were thrown into the sea than for him to cause one of these little ones to stumble." (Luke 17:1-2)

3.2.4 - Do Not Take Oaths (Watch What You Say)

Oaths are not a very common legal process in the Western world these days. An exception is within the court system, where such are often administered to a witness prior to giving evidence in relation to the truth of the testimony they will give (e.g., "I solemnly swear to tell the truth, the whole truth, and nothing but the truth, so help me, God."). In principle, our honesty and integrity should be sufficient to demonstrate that we mean (or will do) what we say:

> Again, you have heard that it was said to our ancestors, You must not break your oath, but you must keep your oaths to the Lord. But I tell you, don't take an oath at all: either by heaven, because it is God's throne; or by the earth, because it is His footstool; or by Jerusalem, because it is the city of the great King. Neither should you swear by your head, because you cannot make a single hair white or black. But let your word "yes" be "yes," and your "no" be "no." Anything more than this is from the evil one. (Matthew 5:33-37).

3.2.5 - Store Up Treasures in Heaven

We should focus on our investment in God's kingdom rather than trying to build wealth for its own sake here on earth:

> Don't collect for yourselves treasures on earth, where moth and rust destroy and where thieves break in and steal. But collect for yourselves treasures in heaven, where neither moth nor rust

---

[15] This term "little ones" can refer to those who are new to or weak in faith, young, or lacking in knowledge and understanding.

destroys, and where thieves don't break in and steal. For where your treasure is, there your heart will be also. (Matthew 6:19-21, NIV)

Sell your possessions and give to the poor. Provide purses for yourselves that will not wear out, a treasure in heaven that will never fail, where no thief comes near and no moth destroys. For where your treasure is, there your heart will be also. (Luke 12:33-34)

3.2.6 - Let Our Light Shine before Others

Our conduct and witness to others should be blameless so that they can see we are really followers of Jesus:

In the same way, let your light shine before men, so that they may see your good works and give glory to your Father in heaven. (Matthew 5:16)

3.2.7 - Rejoice, Including When Being Persecuted

Having an attitude of thankfulness and rejoicing even in the most difficult circumstances can only be a gift from God since we could not do this in our own strength:

You are blessed when they insult and persecute you and falsely say every kind of evil against you because of Me. Be glad and rejoice, because your reward is great in heaven. For that is how they persecuted the prophets who were before you. (Matthew 5:11-12. See also Luke 6:22-23)

However, don't rejoice that the spirits submit to you, but rejoice that your names are written in heaven. (Luke 10:20)

3.3 - Live Out Kingdom Values - (KP5)

Here we look at scriptures underpinning the third Kingdom Practice that correlates to the Kingdom Fundamental to Follow Jesus, which is to Live Out Kingdom Values. This Kingdom Practice is in turn supported by related commands of Jesus that have been grouped into seven distinct Kingdom Behaviours:

- Live honourably.
- Practise giving, praying, and fasting.
- Practise justice, mercy, and faithfulness.
- Give to God what is God's and to authorities and others what is due to them.
- Trust in God's provision and peace.
- Celebrate the Lord's Supper.
- Be ready for Jesus's return/keep watch.

These are described in more detail in subsections 3.3.1 to 3.3.7.

Figure 12 shows the interaction between this Kingdom Practice and the Kingdom Fundamental to Follow Jesus in terms of how we comply personally with Jesus's teachings that centre around obeying and keeping God's moral law.

Figure 12 - Kingdom Practice 5 - to Live Out Kingdom Values

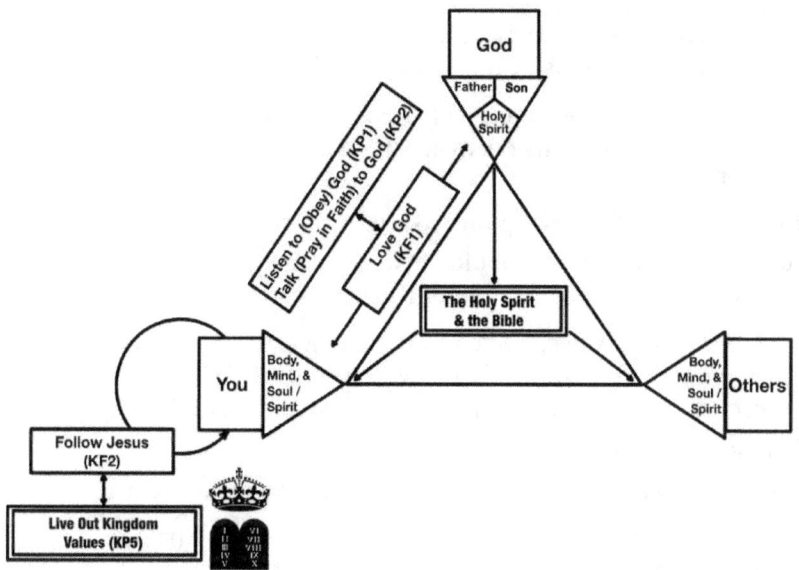

3.3.1 - Live Honourably

Jesus draws our attention to a number of Old Testament commandments that underpin right living for his followers:

Honour God's Law

Jesus makes it clear that he came to live fully by the law and that it still remains as a standard until the end of time. However, we are freed from the penalty for breaking the law because of Jesus's sacrifice:

> Don't assume that I came to destroy the Law or the Prophets. I did not come to destroy but to fulfil. For I assure you: Until heaven and earth pass away, not the smallest letter or one stroke of a letter will pass from the law until all things are accomplished. Therefore, whoever breaks one of the least of these commands and teaches people to do so will be called least in the kingdom of heaven. But whoever practises and teaches these commands will be called great in the kingdom of heaven. (Matthew 5:17-19)

> "Which ones?" he asked Him. Jesus answered: "Do not murder; do not commit adultery; do not steal; do not bear false witness; honour

your father and your mother; and love your neighbour as yourself."
(Matthew 19:18–19, Mark 10:19, Luke 18:20)

Honour Our Parents

We need to respect and honour our parents (note in Deuteronomy 5:16 that this commandment in particular includes a conditional promise from God for those who fulfil it). Naturally, this can be a particularly difficult command for those who have grown up with parents who were abusive or neglected them:

> For God said: Honour your father and your mother; and, the one who speaks evil of father or mother must be put to death. (Matthew 15:4)

Do Not Covet (Guard Against Greed)

Jesus highlights that we should not desire to acquire or own many things, especially those that belong to others:

> Then he said to them, "Watch out! Be on your guard against all kinds of greed; [Some translations say "covetousness"] life does not consist in an abundance of possessions." (Luke 12:15, NIV)

Honour Marriage

We are to hold to our marriage vows if we have made them:

> So they are no longer two, but one flesh. Therefore, what God has joined together, man must not separate. (Matthew 19:6)

> And I tell you, whoever divorces his wife, except for sexual immorality, and marries another, commits adultery. (Matthew 19:9)

Do Not Commit Adultery

Jesus makes it clear that we should not have extramarital relationships or a relationship with a married person if we are single. He also challenges us that adultery is not just a physical act but is first conceived in the mind/heart as lustful thoughts. Consequently, we should aim to maintain mental purity by not allowing or cultivating such ideas (see 2 Corinthians 10:5):

> You have heard that it was said, Do not commit adultery. But I tell you, everyone who looks at a woman to lust for her has already committed adultery with her in his heart. (Matthew 5:27–28)

3.3.2 - Practise Giving, Praying, and Fasting

In Matthew 6:1-18, Jesus gives specific commands about how we are to give. This includes not broadcasting what we have done, praying in secret, and fasting in such a way that others will not notice:

Giving

> Be careful not to practise your righteousness in front of people, to be seen by them. Otherwise, you will have no reward from your Father in heaven. So whenever you give to the poor, don't sound a

trumpet before you, as the hypocrites do in the synagogues and on the streets, to be applauded by people. I assure you: They've got their reward! But when you give to the poor, don't let your left hand know what your right hand is doing, so that your giving may be in secret. And your Father who sees in secret will reward you.

Praying

Whenever you pray, you must not be like the hypocrites, because they love to pray standing in the synagogues and on the street corners to be seen by people. I assure you: They've got their reward! But when you pray, go into your private room, shut your door, and pray to your Father who is in secret. And your Father who sees in secret will reward you. When you pray, don't babble like the idolaters, since they imagine they'll be heard for their many words. Don't be like them, because your Father knows the things you need before you ask Him.

Therefore, you should pray like this: Our Father in heaven, Your name be honoured as holy. Your kingdom come. Your will be done on earth as it is in heaven. Give us today our daily bread. And forgive us our debts, as we also have forgiven our debtors. And do not bring us into temptation, but deliver us from the evil one [For Yours is the kingdom and the power and the glory forever. Amen]. For if you forgive people their wrongdoing, your heavenly Father will forgive you as well. But if you don't forgive people, your Father will not forgive your wrongdoing.

Fasting

Whenever you fast, don't be sad-faced like the hypocrites. For they make their faces unattractive so their fasting is obvious to people. I assure you: They've got their reward! But when you fast, put oil on your head, and wash your face, so that you don't show your fasting to people but to your Father who is in secret. And your Father who sees in secret will reward you.

3.3.3 - Practise Justice, Mercy, and Faithfulness

We are to behave in a way that is just and shows grace and mercy. We are also to be full of faith, which is as important as paying our tithes. Note that Jesus lived in a context where tithing was culturally expected. Views within church groups today differ on whether there is an ongoing requirement for Christians to pay tithes (see 2 Corinthians 9:7). Jesus himself neither reiterated the command to tithe nor explicitly dismissed it as no longer relevant:

Woe to you, scribes and Pharisees, hypocrites! You pay a tenth of mint, dill, and cumin, yet you have neglected the more important matters of the law – justice, mercy, and faith. These things should have been done without neglecting the others. (Matthew 23:23)

3.3.4 - Give to God What is God's and to Authorities and Others What is Due to Them

As part of our duty to our government, we should pay our taxes (however unpalatable!), return to others anything that they have loaned to us (money or other things), and give to God what he asks of us:

> "Show Me the coin used for the tax." So they brought Him a denarius. "Whose image and inscription is this?" He asked them. "Caesar's," they said to Him. Then He said to them, "Therefore give back to Caesar the things that are Caesar's, and to God the things that are God's." (Matthew 22:19-21. See also Mark 12:17, Luke 20:25)

3.3.5 - Trust in God's Provision and Peace

Jesus offers each of us his peace, an inner peace that is different from peace as the world understands it and upon which we can draw when things become difficult:

> This is why I tell you: Don't worry about your life, what you will eat or what you will drink; or about your body, what you will wear. Isn't life more than food and the body more than clothing? Look at the birds of the sky: They don't sow or reap or gather into barns, yet your heavenly Father feeds them. Aren't you worth more than they? (Matthew 6:25-26)

> Peace I leave with you. My peace I give to you. I do not give to you as the world gives. Your heart must not be troubled or fearful. (John 14:27)

> I have told you these things so that in Me you may have peace. You will have suffering in this world. Be courageous! I have conquered the world. (John 16:33)

3.3.6 - Celebrate the Lord's Supper

We are to regularly remember Jesus by celebrating the sacrament of the Lord's Supper, which he specifically instituted before his crucifixion:

> As they were eating, Jesus took bread, blessed and broke it, gave it to the disciples, and said, "Take and eat it; this is My body." Then He took a cup, and after giving thanks, He gave it to them and said, "Drink from it, all of you." (Matthew 26:26-27)

> Then He took a cup, and after giving thanks, He said, "Take this and share it among yourselves. For I tell you, from now on I will not drink of the fruit of the vine until the kingdom of God comes." And He took bread, gave thanks, broke it, gave it to them, and said, "This is My body, which is given for you. Do this in remembrance of Me". In the same way He also took the cup after supper and said, "This cup is

the new covenant established by My blood; it is shed for you." (Luke 22:17-20)

3.3.7 - Be Ready for Jesus's Return/Keep Watch

The Bible tells us that the end of the age "will come like a thief" (2 Peter 3:10), so we are to be ready for Jesus's return. There are many theories and interpretations about the signs of the times and what and when this will happen. However, the Bible says:

> Therefore be alert, since you don't know what day your Lord is coming. But know this: If the homeowner had known what time the thief was coming, he would have stayed alert and not let his house be broken into. This is why you also must be ready, because the Son of Man is coming at an hour you do not expect. (Matthew 24:42-44)

> Therefore be alert, because you don't know either the day or the hour. (Matthew 25:13)

> Now concerning that day or hour no one knows –neither the angels in heaven nor the Son –except the Father. Watch! Be alert! For you don't know when the time is coming. It is like a man on a journey, who left his house, gave authority to his slaves, gave each one his work, and commanded the doorkeeper to be alert. Therefore be alert, since you don't know when the master of the house is coming –whether in the evening or at midnight or at the crowing of the rooster or early in the morning. Otherwise, he might come suddenly and find you sleeping. And what I say to you, I say to everyone: Be alert. (Mark 13:32-37)

> Be ready for service and have your lamps lit. You must be like people waiting for their master to return from the wedding banquet so that when he comes and knocks, they can open the door for him at once. Those slaves the master will find alert when he comes will be blessed. I assure you: He will get ready, have them recline at the table, then come and serve them. If he comes in the middle of the night, or even near dawn, and finds them alert, those slaves are blessed. But know this: If the homeowner had known at what hour the thief was coming, he would not have let his house be broken into. You also be ready, because the Son of Man is coming at an hour that you do not expect. (Luke 12:35-40)

> Then He told the disciples: "The days are coming when you will long to see one of the days of the Son of Man, but you won't see it. They will say to you, "Look there!" or "Look here!" Don't follow or run after them. For as the lightning flashes from horizon to horizon and lights up the sky, so the Son of Man will be in His day. But first He must suffer many things and be rejected by this generation." (Luke 17:22-25)

> Then He said, "Watch out that you are not deceived. For many will come in My name, saying, "I am He," and, "The time is near." Don't

follow them. When you hear of wars and rebellions, don't be alarmed. Indeed, these things must take place first, but the end won't come right away." (Luke 21:8-9)

Look! I am coming quickly, and My reward is with Me to repay each person according to what he has done. I am the Alpha and the Omega, the First and the Last, the Beginning and the End. Blessed are those who wash their robes, so that they may have the right to the tree of life and may enter the city by the gates. (Revelation 22:12-14)

3.4 - Exercise Discernment - (KP6)

This subsection presents the scriptures underpinning the fourth Kingdom Practice that correlates to the Kingdom Fundamental to Follow Jesus, which is to Exercise Discernment. This Kingdom Practice is in turn supported by related commands of Jesus that have been grouped into five distinct Kingdom Behaviours:

- Guard against falsehood.
- Do not be deceived.
- Be wise as serpents and innocent as doves.
- Do not throw our pearls to pigs.
- Do not blaspheme against the Holy Spirit.

Subsections 3.4.1 to 3.4.5 set out the scriptures that support each individual Kingdom Behaviour.

The relationship perspective is shown in Figure 13.

Figure 13 - Kingdom Practice 6 - to Exercise Discernment

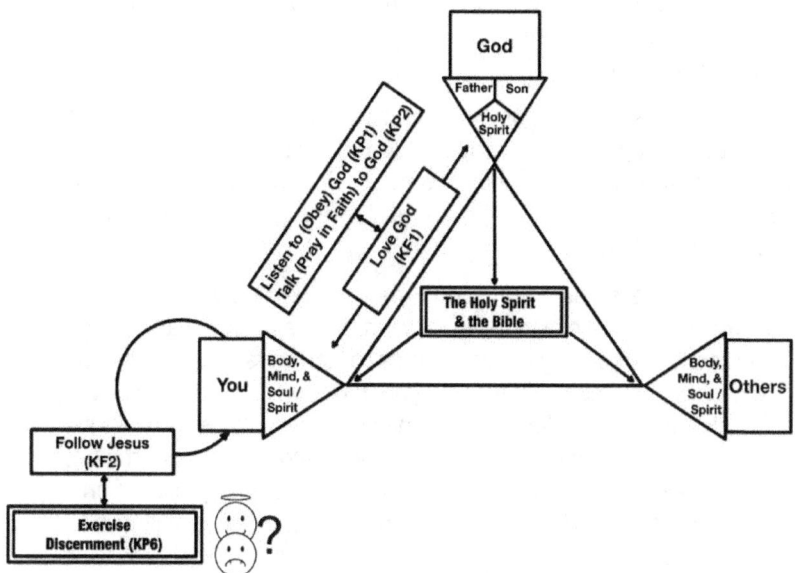

3.4.1 - Guard against Falsehood

As followers of Jesus, we are warned that we should test whether we are being misled by our spiritual leaders. How they live will be a true indicator of where their hearts really lie as these supporting Kingdom Behaviours indicate.

Beware of False Teaching.

We need to check that those who teach and disciple us are being true to God's Word:

> Why is it you don't understand that when I told you, "Beware of the yeast of the Pharisees and Sadducees," it wasn't about bread? Then they understood that He did not tell them to beware of the yeast in bread, but of the teaching of the Pharisees and Sadducees. (Matthew 16:11-12. See also Matthew 16:6)

Beware of False Prophets.

Similarly, we should be checking whether those who claim to be God's messengers truly are. We can do this by looking at their fruit and seeing if their lives are consistent with what they say:

> Beware of false prophets who come to you in sheep's clothing but inwardly are ravaging wolves. You'll recognise them by their fruit. Are grapes gathered from thorn bushes or figs from thistles? In the same way, every good tree produces good fruit, but a bad tree produces bad fruit. A good tree can't produce bad fruit; neither can

a bad tree produce good fruit. Every tree that doesn't produce good fruit is cut down and thrown into the fire. So you'll recognise them by their fruit. (Matthew 7:15-20)

3.4.2 - Do Not Be Deceived

The Bible tells us how Jesus will return (1 Thessalonians 4:13-18). This means that any alternative message in contradiction of Scripture is false and we are being deceived if we believe it. If what we are being told does not conform with Scripture and its reasonable interpretation, then it should be scrutinised very closely:

> If anyone tells you then, "Look, here is the Messiah!" or, "Over here!" do not believe it! False messiahs and false prophets will arise and perform great signs and wonders to lead astray, if possible, even the elect. Take note: I have told you in advance. So if they tell you, "Look, He's in the wilderness!" don't go out; "Look, He's in the inner rooms!" do not believe it. For as the lightning comes from the east and flashes as far as the west, so will be the coming of the Son of Man. Wherever the carcass is, there the vultures will gather. (Matthew 24:23-28. See also Matthew 24:4-5, Mark 13:5-9, Mark 13:20-23)

3.4.3 - Be as Wise as Serpents and Innocent as Doves

Jesus expects us to use our ingenuity and shrewdness when dealing with non-believers, but in a way that is not sinful or dishonouring to him or the gospel message:

> Look, I'm sending you out like sheep among wolves. Therefore be as shrewd as serpents and as harmless as doves. (Matthew 10:16)

3.4.4 - Do Not Throw Our Pearls to Pigs

This warning is specifically not to share the gospel and things of God with those who are strongly antagonistic or likely to be potentially violent upon hearing the message (e.g. an angry crowd):

> Don't give what is holy to dogs or toss your pearls before pigs, or they will trample them with their feet, turn, and tear you to pieces. (Matthew 7:6)

3.4.5 - Do Not Blaspheme against the Holy Spirit

We are specifically warned that we should not defame the Holy Spirit or attribute the work of the Holy Spirit to any other power. We must therefore be discerning to ensure that we can recognise fully when God is at work. We have the Holy Spirit within us to bear witness to us when this is the case, but only if we choose to listen to him:

> "But whoever blasphemes against the Holy Spirit never has forgiveness, but is guilty of an eternal sin" – because they were

saying, "He has an unclean spirit." (Mark 3:29-30. See also Luke 12:10).

In effect, this means neither recognising God at work nor giving him the glory, instead attributing the outcome of God's working to other forces. This is what the Pharisees did in accusing Jesus of being in league with Satan/demons[16]. In doing so, they were explicitly rejecting Jesus, God, and the Holy Spirit.

Let me hasten to add here that if we as Christians feel we have misattributed God being at work or perhaps even have not been spiritually aware to recognise the working of the Holy Spirit, this does not imply we are guilty of blasphemy, therefore beyond forgiveness. Unintentional ignorance or error is completely different from a deliberate and total rejection of God. Nor does God expect us to be spiritually perfect or mature overnight. Consequently, in such instances we should not come under condemnation or feel there is no forgiveness for us:

> Therefore, there is now no condemnation for those who are in Christ Jesus. (Romans 8:1, NIV)

> For I am convinced that neither death nor life, neither angels nor demons, neither the present nor the future, nor any powers, neither height nor depth, nor anything else in all creation, will be able to separate us from the love of God that is in Christ Jesus our Lord. (Romans 8:38-39, NIV)

> If we claim to be without sin, we deceive ourselves and the truth is not in us. If we confess our sins, he is faithful and just and will forgive us our sins and purify us from all unrighteousness. If we claim we have not sinned, we make him out to be a liar and his word is not in us. (1 John 1:8-10, NIV)

---

[16] We should note that there are different interpretations concerning what "blaspheming against the Holy Spirit" means in today's context, so not all will understand this in the way described here.

Chapter 4 - Love Your Neighbour as Yourself - (KF3)

Chapter 3 presented the biblical foundation for the Kingdom Fundamental to Follow Jesus and its four supporting Kingdom Practices. In this chapter we will consider the third and final Kingdom Fundamental stemming from the instruction Jesus gave his followers to "teach them all that I have commanded you," which is to Love Your Neighbour as Yourself (see Figure 2). This Kingdom Fundamental is underscored by Jesus himself in the same discussion in which he identifies the two "greatest commandments", the first of which we've already identified as our first Kingdom Fundamental:

> The second is: "Love your neighbour as yourself. There is no other command greater than these." (Mark 12:31. See also Matthew 22:39)

Jesus gives at least two other commands to love specific groups of people.

Love One Another

One very specific command from Jesus is for us to love our fellow followers of him:

> I give you a new command: Love one another. Just as I have loved you, you must also love one another. By this all people will know that you are My disciples, if you have love for one another. (John 13:34-35)

While this is simply one particular instance of loving your neighbour as yourself, Jesus singles it out as a specific requirement for his followers:

This is what I command you: Love one another. (John 15:17)

Love Your Enemies

He also commanded us to love our enemies, a challenge that is counter-cultural regardless of where we live on this planet:

> But I say to you who listen: Love your enemies, do what is good to those who hate you, bless those who curse you, pray for those who mistreat you. If anyone hits you on the cheek, offer the other also. And if anyone takes away your coat, don't hold back your shirt either. (Luke 6:27-29. See also Matthew 5:44)

> But love your enemies, do what is good, and lend, expecting nothing in return. Then your reward will be great, and you will be sons of the Most High. For He is gracious to the ungrateful and evil. (Luke 6:35)

The commands of Jesus that centre around this Kingdom Fundamental can be grouped into three Kingdom Practices:

- Make disciples.
- Forgive (don't judge) others.
- Undertake acts of service/generosity.

Each of these Kingdom Practices is supported by a number of supporting Kingdom Behaviours, as you can see in the centre and right-hand side of Figure 14. These Kingdom Behaviours are described individually in subsections 4.1 to 4.3.

Figure 14 - The Kingdom Practices and Kingdom Behaviours That Underpin Kingdom Fundamental 3 - to Love Your Neighbour as Yourself

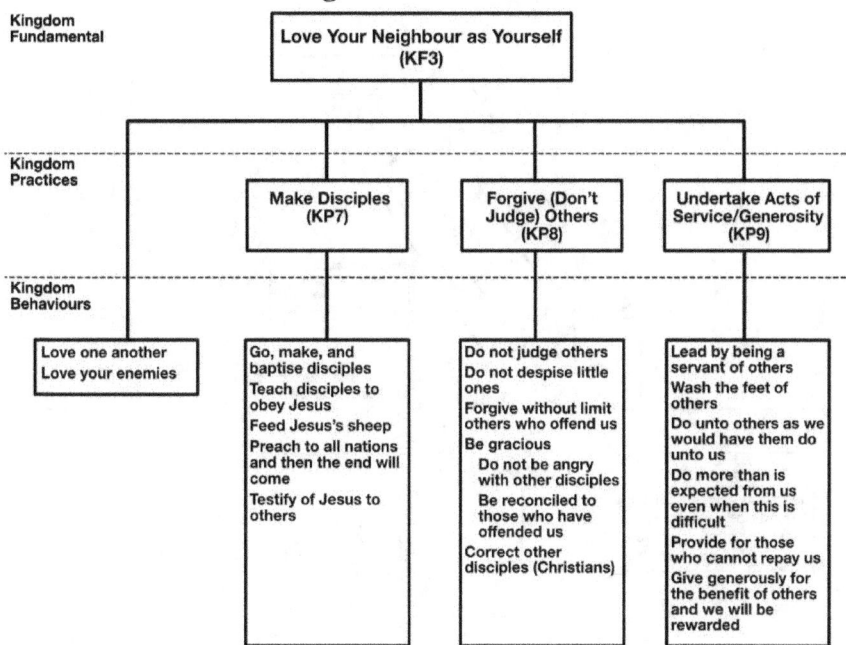

If we look at this relationally, Figure 15 seeks to show this in terms of our ongoing interactions with other people, whoever they may be.

Figure 15 - Kingdom Fundamental 3 - to Love Your Neighbour as Yourself

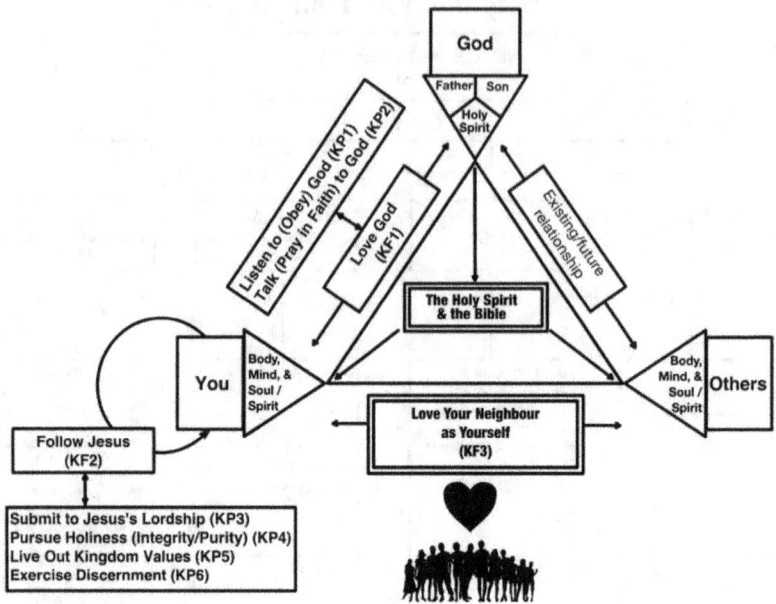

4.1 - Make Disciples - (KP7)

Now that we've considered what Jesus means by loving our neighbour, we can consider those scriptures that give an underpinning to the first Kingdom Practice that correlates to the Kingdom Fundamental to Love Your Neighbour as Yourself, which is to Make Disciples. Commands of Jesus related to this Kingdom Practice have been grouped into five distinct Kingdom Behaviours:

- Go, make, and baptise disciples.
- Teach disciples to obey Jesus.
- Feed Jesus's sheep.
- Preach to all nations, and then the end will come.
- Testify of Jesus to others.

These are described in more detail in subsections 4.1.1 to 4.1.5.

Figure 16 demonstrates this relationally.

Figure 16 - Kingdom Practice 7 - to Make Disciples

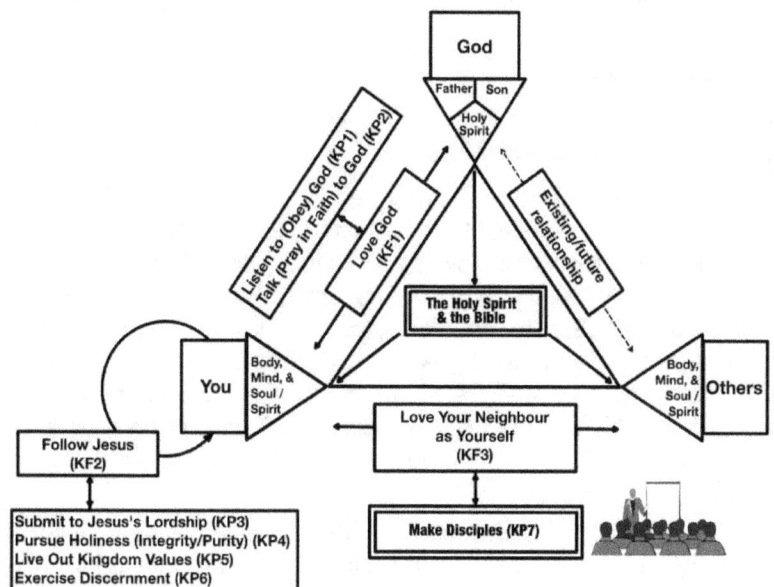

4.1.1 - Go, Make, and Baptise Disciples

Sharing our love of Jesus with others is a command to every follower of Jesus. This necessitates relying upon the Holy Spirit to convict others of their need for Jesus and to bring them to repentance:

> Go, therefore, and make disciples of all nations, baptising them in the name of the Father and of the Son and of the Holy Spirit. (Matthew 28:19)

> Then He said to them, "Go into all the world and preach the gospel to the whole creation. Whoever believes and is baptised will be saved, but whoever does not believe will be condemned. And these signs will accompany those who believe: In My name they will drive out demons; they will speak in new languages; they will pick up snakes; if they should drink anything deadly, it will never harm them; they will lay hands on the sick, and they will get well." Then after speaking to them, the Lord Jesus was taken up into heaven and sat down at the right hand of God. And they went out and preached everywhere, the Lord working with them and confirming the word by the accompanying signs. (Mark 16:15-20)

4.1.2 - Teach Disciples to Obey Jesus

We are to train and instruct new and existing followers so that they grow in their faith and in the practice of Jesus's commands:

teaching them to observe everything I have commanded you. And remember, I am with you always, to the end of the age. (Matthew 28:20)

4.1.3 - Feed Jesus's Sheep

This is another way of describing the need to help others grow in their relationship with God in Jesus:

> When they had eaten breakfast, Jesus asked Simon Peter, "Simon, son of John, do you love Me more than these?" "Yes, Lord," he said to Him, "You know that I love You." "Feed My lambs," He told him. A second time He asked him, "Simon, son of John, do you love Me?" "Yes, Lord," he said to Him, "You know that I love You". "Shepherd My sheep," He told him. He asked him the third time, "Simon, son of John, do you love Me?" Peter was grieved that He asked him the third time, "Do you love Me?" He said, "Lord, You know everything! You know that I love You." "Feed My sheep," Jesus said. (John 21:15-17)

This text comes after Peter's three denials of Jesus that followed Jesus's arrest. In this encounter, we see Jesus lovingly restoring Peter as he still does for any repentant follower time and again, no matter what we have done or how greatly we have failed. To each of Peter's three denials, Jesus offered three corresponding encouragements to move Peter forward from his failure and guilt.

This passage begs several questions. Was the command to "feed my sheep" just for Peter, or are all of us called to help others in their discipleship? If we are disciples who are to make disciples, then shouldn't we be feeding Jesus's sheep too?

4.1.4 - Preach to All Nations and Then the End Will Come

Jesus's words below give assurance that once we have shared the gospel with all people groups and they have been given opportunity to respond, then Jesus will return:

> And this gospel of the kingdom shall be preached in all the world for a witness unto all nations; and then shall the end come. (Matthew 24:14, NIV)

> And the good news must first be proclaimed to all nations. (Mark 13:10)

4.1.5 - Testify of Jesus to Others

While not strictly a command, Jesus implies in the following text that part of being his follower is testifying to others about him:

> When the Counsellor comes, the One I will send to you from the Father – the Spirit of truth who proceeds from the Father – He will

testify about Me. You also will testify, because you have been with Me from the beginning. (John 15:26-27)

4.2 - Forgive (Don't Judge) Others - (KP8)

Here we look at the scriptures supporting the second Kingdom Practice that correlates to the Kingdom Fundamental to Love Your Neighbour as Yourself, which is to Forgive (Don't Judge) Others. Commands of Jesus underpinning this Kingdom Practice have been grouped into five distinct Kingdom Behaviours:

- Do not judge others.
- Do not despise little ones.
- Forgive without limit others who offend us.
- Be gracious.
- Correct other disciples (Christians).

These are amplified in subsections 4.2.1 to 4.2.5.

Figure 17 illustrates this relationally.

Figure 17 - Kingdom Practice 8 - to Forgive (Don't Judge) Others

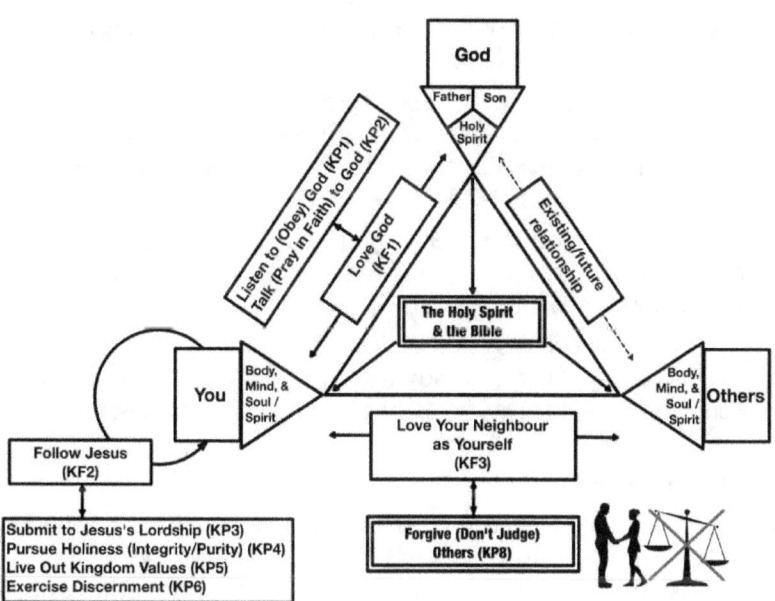

4.2.1 - Do Not Judge Others

Jesus tells us that we must not judge other people. This applies especially to those outside God's kingdom as they will generally not have any real understanding of what God wants from them. Because we are not perfect, we are not in a position to assess the behaviour of others (e.g. the account of the woman caught in adultery in John 8:3-11):

> Do not judge, so that you won't be judged. For with the judgement you use, you will be judged, and with the measure you use, it will be measured to you. (Matthew 7:1-2)

> Do not judge, and you will not be judged. Do not condemn, and you will not be condemned. Forgive, and you will be forgiven. (Luke 6:37)

4.2.2 - Do Not Despise Little Ones

Essentially, Jesus is telling us not to look down on (be contemptuous of) those who are new to or weak in faith, young, or lacking in knowledge and understanding. Instead we should seek to build them up:

> See that you don't look down on one of these little ones, because I tell you that in heaven their angels continually view the face of My Father in heaven. (Matthew 18:10)

4.2.3 - Forgive without Limit Others Who Offend Us

We should continue forgiving when others ask us for forgiveness so that we will be forgiven ourselves:

> For if you forgive other people when they sin against you, your heavenly Father will also forgive you. But if you do not forgive others their sins, your Father will not forgive your sins. (Matthew 6:14-15, NIV)

> Then Peter came to Him and said, "Lord, how many times could my brother sin against me and I forgive him? As many as seven times?" "I tell you, not as many as seven," Jesus said to him, "but 70 times seven." (Matthew 18:21-22)

> And whenever you stand praying, if you have anything against anyone, forgive him, so that your Father in heaven will also forgive you your wrongdoing. (Mark 11:25)

> Be on your guard. If your brother sins, rebuke him, and if he repents, forgive him. And if he sins against you seven times in a day, and comes back to you seven times, saying, "I repent," you must forgive him. (Luke 17:3-4)

4.2.4 - Be Gracious

As followers of Jesus, we need to extend the grace we have received from God in Christ for the forgiveness of our sins to others who have wronged us. In terms of Jesus's commands, the following supporting Kingdom Behaviours tell us what he needs us to do:

Do Not be Angry with Other Disciples

We are to adopt an attitude of patience and perseverance with fellow believers, accepting their limitations and faults as we also have our own weaknesses:

> But I tell you that anyone who is angry with a brother or sister will be subject to judgment. Again, anyone who says to a brother or sister, 'Raca,' is answerable to the court. And anyone who says, 'You fool!' will be in danger of the fire of hell. (Matthew 5:22, NIV)

Be Reconciled to Those Who Have Offended Us

If we hold something against another person, we need to release them in forgiveness so that we can be right before God:

> So if you are offering your gift on the altar, and there you remember that your brother has something against you, leave your gift there in front of the altar. First go and be reconciled with your brother, and then come and offer your gift. Reach a settlement quickly with your adversary while you're on the way with him, or your adversary will hand you over to the judge, the judge to the officer, and you will be thrown into prison. (Matthew 5:23-25. See also Luke 12:58-59)

4.2.5 - Correct Other Disciples (Christians)

Jesus gives explicit instructions for how to manage persistent sin and wrongdoing within his church. He provides an escalatory process for challenging and encouraging one of the fellowship to come into line with living righteously:

> If your brother sins against you, go and rebuke him in private. If he listens to you, you have won your brother. But if he won't listen, take one or two more with you, so that by the testimony of two or three witnesses every fact may be established. If he pays no attention to them, tell the church. But if he doesn't pay attention even to the church, let him be like an unbeliever and a tax collector to you. (Matthew 18:15-17)

4.3 - Undertake Acts of Service/Generosity - (KP9)

This subsection identifies the scriptures that provide the basis for the third Kingdom Practice that correlates to the Kingdom Fundamental to Love Your Neighbour as Yourself, which is to Undertake Acts of Service/Generosity. Related commands of Jesus that support this Kingdom Practice have been grouped into six distinct Kingdom Behaviours:

- Lead by being a servant of others.
- Wash the feet of others.
- Do unto others as we would have them do unto us.
- Do more than is expected from us even when this is difficult.

- Provide for those who cannot repay us.
- Give generously for the benefit of others, and we will be rewarded.

Underpinning scriptures for each of these are set out in subsections 4.3.1 to 4.3.6 below. The relationship perspective is shown in Figure 18.

Figure 18 - Kingdom Practice 9 - to Undertake Acts of Service/Generosity

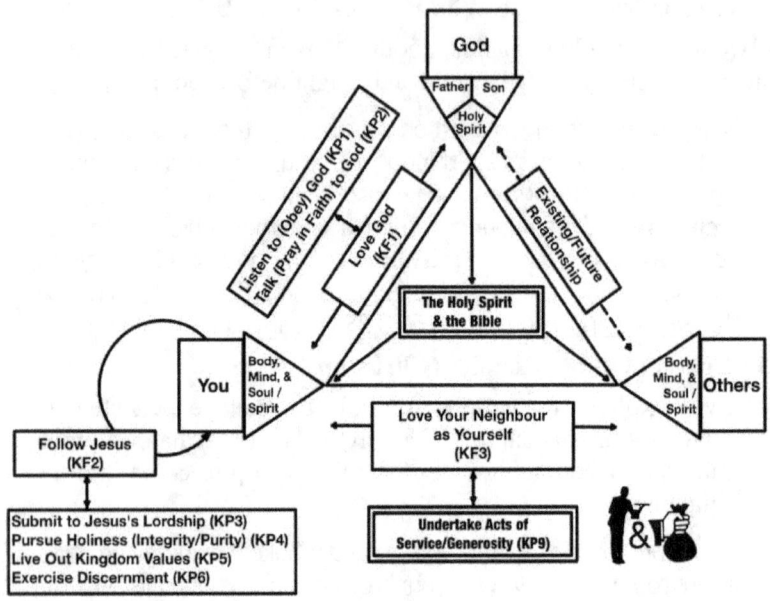

4.3.1 - Lead by Being a Servant of Others

As followers of Jesus, we shouldn't adopt the world's accepted method of seeking power and authority as the mark of leadership. Instead, we are to lead by offering ourselves in service to those around us:

> It must not be like that among you. On the contrary, whoever wants to become great among you must be your servant, and whoever wants to be first among you must be your slave; just as the Son of Man did not come to be served, but to serve, and to give His life – a ransom for many. (Matthew 20:26-28. See also Mark 10:44-45)

> Sitting down, He called the Twelve and said to them, "If anyone wants to be first, he must be last of all and servant of all." (Mark 9:35)

> But when you are invited, go and recline in the lowest place, so that when the one who invited you comes, he will say to you, "Friend, move up higher." You will then be honoured in the presence of all

the other guests. For everyone who exalts himself will be humbled, and the one who humbles himself will be exalted. (Luke 14:10-11)

Then a dispute also arose among them about who should be considered the greatest. But He said to them, "The kings of the Gentiles dominate them, and those who have authority over them are called 'Benefactors.' But it must not be like that among you. On the contrary, whoever is greatest among you must become like the youngest, and whoever leads, like the one serving." (Luke 22:24-26)

4.3.2 - Wash the Feet of Others

Although not a common practice these days in industrialized nations, the process of foot washing is effectively saying that we should be prepared to serve others, even when this might be unpleasant or humbling for us:

So if I, your Lord and Teacher, have washed your feet, you also ought to wash one another's feet. (John 13:14)

4.3.3 - Do unto Others as We Would Have Them Do to Us

We should adopt a mind-set that seeks to relate to others in a God-honouring way, treating them how we would like to be treated:

Therefore, whatever you want others to do for you, do also the same for them – this is the Law and the Prophets. (Matthew 7:12. See also Luke 6:31).

4.3.4 - Do More than Is Expected from Us Even When This Is Difficult

Jesus uses examples from the Old Testament and life under Roman occupation to illustrate that as his disciples we should exceed the expectations of those around us, being especially generous with our time, resources (e.g. money), and energy:

You have heard that it was said, An eye for an eye and a tooth for a tooth. But I tell you, don't resist an evildoer. On the contrary, if anyone slaps you on your right cheek, turn the other to him also. As for the one who wants to sue you and take away your shirt, let him have your coat as well. And if anyone forces you to go one mile, go with him two. (Matthew 5:38-41)

4.3.5 - Provide for Those Who Cannot Repay Us

Jesus wants us to use our worldly wealth to bless those who have no means to return the favour, i.e., the underprivileged and weakest in society:

He also said to the one who had invited Him, "When you give a lunch or a dinner, don't invite your friends, your brothers, your relatives, or your rich neighbours, because they might invite you back, and you would be repaid. On the contrary, when you host a banquet, invite those who are poor, maimed, lame, or blind. And you will be blessed, because they cannot repay you; for you will be repaid at the resurrection of the righteous." (Luke 14:12-14)

4.3.6 - Give Generously for the Benefit of Others and We Will Be Rewarded

This command to give generously is so that we can share those things with which God has blessed us with others, not with the ulterior motive of receiving even more back (the erroneous prosperity gospel):

> Give to the one who asks you, and don't turn away from the one who wants to borrow from you. (Matthew 5:42)

> Give to everyone who asks you, and from one who takes your things, don't ask for them back. (Luke 6:30)

> Give, and it will be given to you; a good measure – pressed down, shaken together, and running over – will be poured into your lap. For with the measure you use, it will be measured back to you. (Luke 6:38)

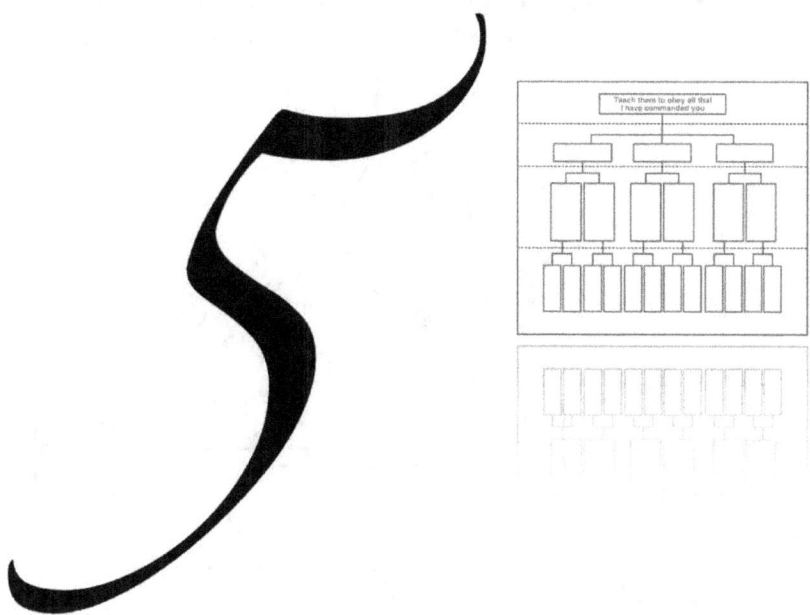

Chapter 5 - Analysis Reflections

As we look back at Chapters 2 to 4, we see that all of the specific commands of Jesus can be classified and grouped into a structure that consists of three Kingdom Fundamentals supported by a total of nine Kingdom Practices. In taking a close look at these Kingdom Practices, we have also ascertained that each one is supported by additional related commands of Jesus, referred to here as Kingdom Behaviours. Organising and grouping these commands into the three descending levels of Kingdom Fundamentals, Kingdom Practices, and Kingdom Behaviours that we have covered in this material has been done with the objective of helping us understand exactly what Jesus taught. Only once we know what Jesus taught can we teach others "to obey everything that I [Jesus] have commanded you" (Matthew 28:20).

This organisational structure can also form the basis for how we might share Jesus's teaching with other disciples to help them understand what Jesus wants each of us to put into practice. The complete set of Kingdom Fundamentals and Kingdom Practices in terms of our relationship with God, with others, and our own personal development aspirations are illustrated in Figure 19.

This analysis represents just one of any number of ways in which scholars or any person with sufficient interest might choose to classify and organise the teachings and commands of Jesus to all his disciples. There is no single right or wrong way to analyse or categorise this material. As a reader, you might consider grouping the commands of Jesus in different ways that could yield alternative sets of Kingdom Practices.

Figure 19 - The Kingdom Fundamentals and Kingdom Practices Jesus Wants Us to Practise and to Teach to Other Followers

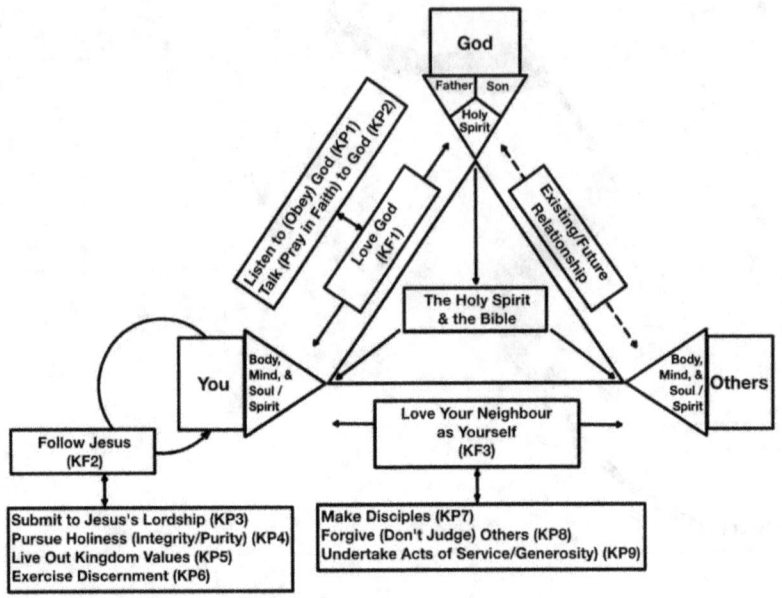

A complete set of Kingdom Fundamentals, Kingdom Practices, and Kingdom Behaviours can be seen in Figure 20 with a different representation of the Kingdom Fundamentals and Kingdom Practices in Figure 21.

Chapter 5 – Analysis Reflections

Figure 20 - The Complete Set of Kingdom Fundamentals, Kingdom Practices, and Kingdom Behaviours Drawn from Jesus's Commands

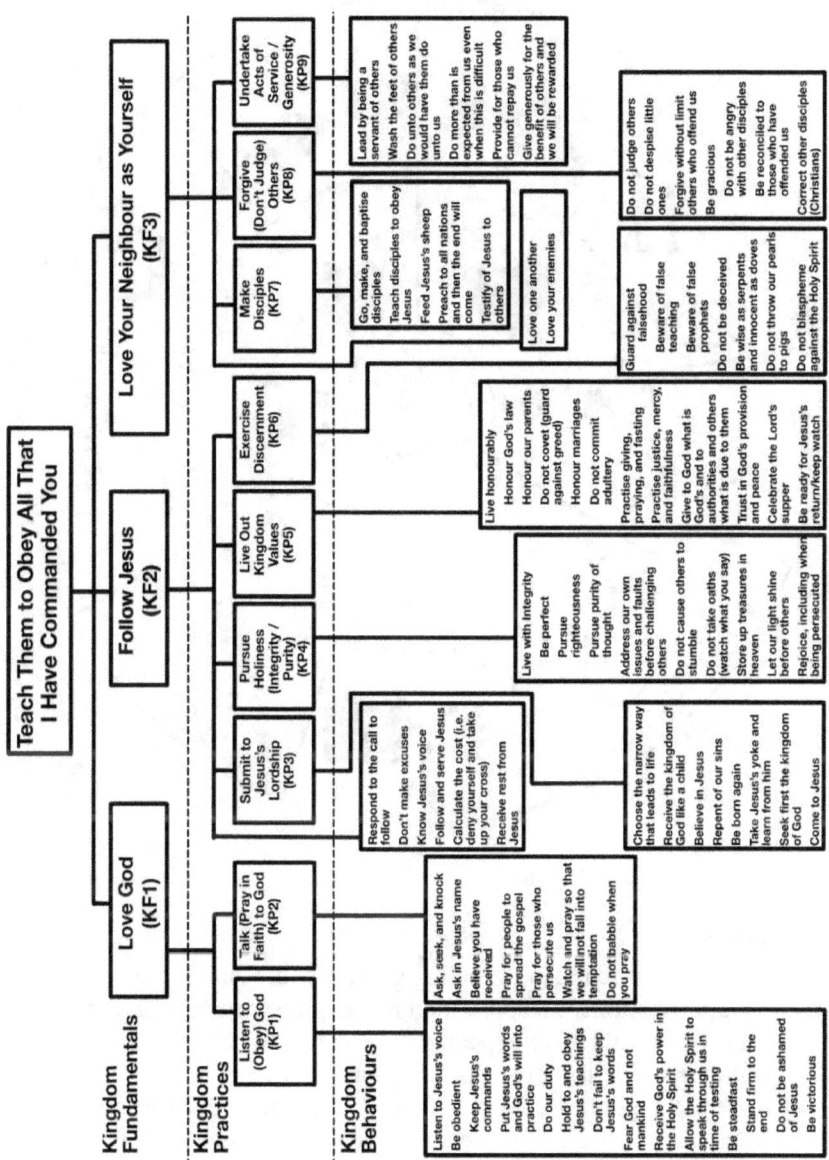

Figure 21 - The Complete Set of Kingdom Fundamentals and Kingdom Practices

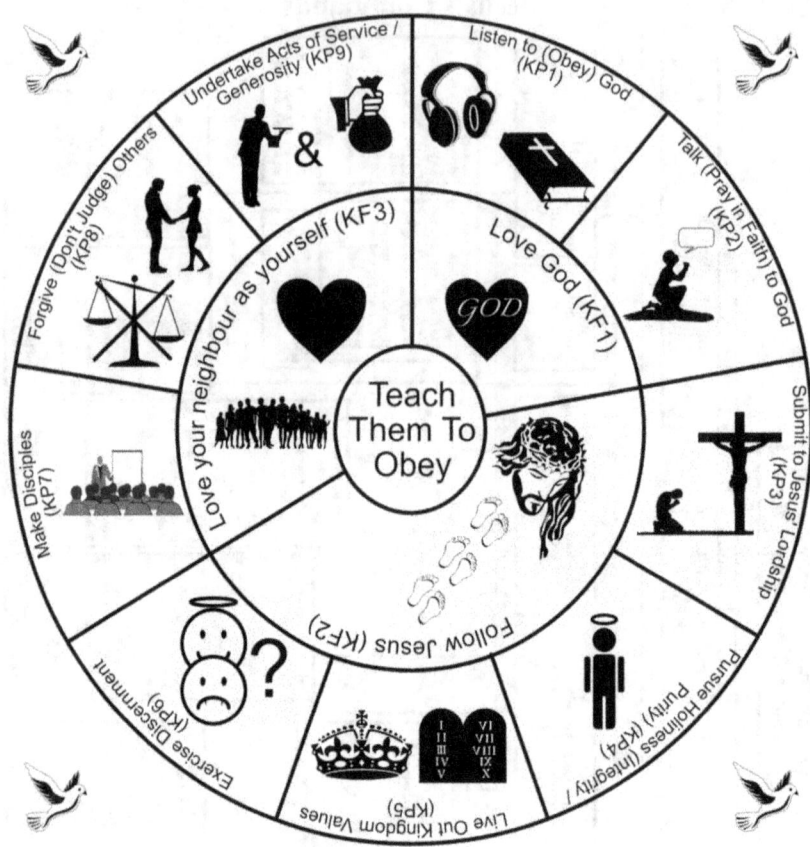

Questions

> What is your reaction to the Kingdom Fundamentals and Kingdom Practices as presented in Chapters 2 to 4? Are they what you would have expected? If you had to choose an alternative title for any of these, what would they be?

> Are the Kingdom Behaviours, which were developed from Jesus's commands, consistent with Jesus's teaching as you understand it?

> If you were creating your own structure, would you organise these Kingdom Behaviours under the same Kingdom Practices and Kingdom Fundamentals (or your alternative

terms) as set out in the material presented here? If not, what might you change?

It is important to understand that Jesus did not define or specifically identify many of the Kingdom Practices presented here by the particular terminology used in this study. That said, Jesus did direct his followers in the Great Commission (Matthew 28:19-20) that when we are making disciples we should teach them to obey all that he has commanded. This analysis and organisational structure here is one possible framework that can be used for sharing the teachings and commands of Jesus with both new and established believers.

Organising Jesus's commands into a structure of three Kingdom Fundamentals and nine Kingdom Practices may make his teachings easier to recall and understand. But let me make clear that will not necessarily make them easier to implement. We still face the daily choice and challenge of living our lives for Jesus and the kingdom of God as best we can. Or conversely choosing to live instead for ourselves, family, and friends.

If we are serious about wanting to be Jesus's disciples, then we have to understand the implications of his commands and how to determine his will for our lives. The corresponding *Studies for Disciples* book can help with that process as it takes each of the elements mentioned in this book (Kingdom Fundamentals, Kingdom Practices, and Kingdom Behaviours) and examines in much greater depth what they mean to our daily Christian growth as well as our call to teach and disciple others.

Appendix 1 – Further Reading on Discipleship

Space within this book has been limited in order to make the material manageable. For those wanting to look deeper into the implications of being a follower of Jesus, it would be worthwhile to consider other bodies of work that focus on the principles of discipleship and the commands of Jesus in particular. Some examples are provided below:

- *What Jesus Demands from the World* by John Piper
- *Celebration of Discipline: The Path to Spiritual Growth* by Richard J. Foster
- *Discipleship* by David Watson
- *Discipleship: Living the Fifty Commands of Christ* by Leah Ramirez
- *Hear Him! the One Hundred Twenty-Five Commands of Jesus* by Peter Wittstock
- *The Commands of Christ: What It Really Means to Follow Jesus* by Tom Blackaby
- *The Great and Beautiful God, The Great and Beautiful Life*, and *The Great and Beautiful Community*, three excellent books by James Bryan Smith

- *The Great Omission: Jesus' Essential Teaching on Discipleship* – Dallas Willard
- *Disciples are Made Not Born* by Walter Hendrichson
- *The Lost Art of Disciple Making* by LeRoy Eims

Other sources that list different numbers of commands of Jesus include the following references (in addition to further searches that can be made on the internet):

- "The Fifty Commands of Jesus" by Matthew Robert Payne - http://ezinearticles.com/?The-Fifty-Commands-of-Jesus&id=468177
- "The Commandments of Jesus" by JS McConnell - http://www.earthsite.org/commandments.htm
- http://aplaceforyou.org/upload/Commands-of-Christ_2017.pdf
- http://www.historymakers.info/sermons/50-commands-of-christ.html

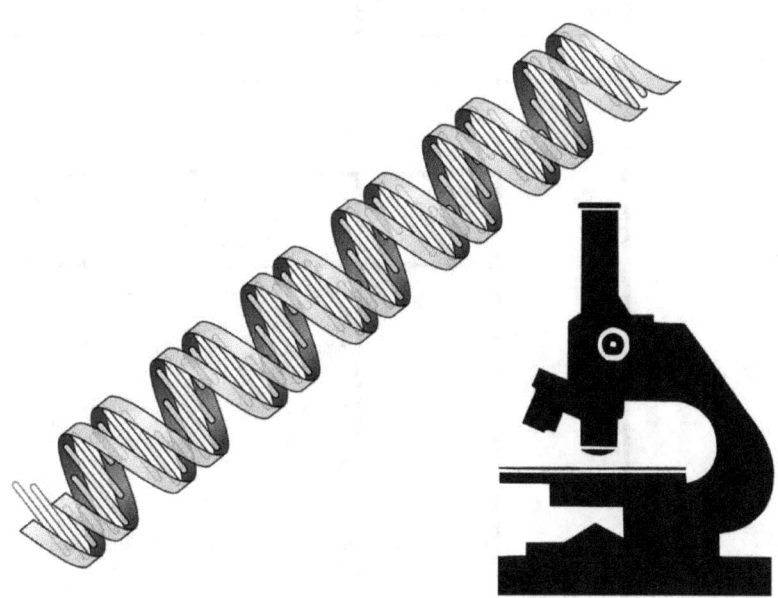

Appendix 2 - Summary of the Biblical Analysis

Kingdom Fundamental	Kingdom Practice	Kingdom Behaviour	Commands & Bible References
Love God			Mark 12:30, Matthew 22:37-38
	Listen to (obey) God		
		Listen to Jesus's voice	Matthew 11:15, Matthew 13:9, Matthew 13:43, Mark 4:9, Mark 4:23, Luke 8:8, Luke 10:16, Luke 14:34-35
		Be obedient	Keep Jesus's commands - John 14:15 Put Jesus's words and God's will into practice - Matthew 7:21, Matthew 7:24-25, Luke 6:46-49 Do Our Duty - Luke 17:7-10 Hold to and obey Jesus's teachings - John 8:31-32, John 8:51, John 14:23-24 Don't fail to keep Jesus's words - John 12:47-48
		Fear God and not mankind	Matthew 10:28, Luke 12:4-5
		Receive God's power in the Holy Spirit	Luke 24:49, John 14:26, John 20:22-23, Acts 1:8
		Allow the Holy Spirit to speak through us in time or testing	Matthew 10:19-20, Mark 13:11, Luke 12:11-12
		Be steadfast	Stand firm to the end - Matthew 10:22-23, Matthew 24:13, Mark 13:13 Do not be ashamed of Jesus - Mark 8:38, Luke 9:26, Luke 12:8-9 Be victorious - Revelation 2:7, Revelation 2:11, Revelation 2:17, Revelation 2:26-28, Revelation 3:5, Revelation 3:12, Revelation 3:21

Teach Them To Obey – All That I Have Commanded You – Appendix 2

Kingdom Fundamental	Kingdom Practice	Kingdom Behaviour	Commands & Bible References
Love God	Talk (pray in faith) to God		
		Ask, seek, and knock	Matthew 7:7-8, Luke 11:9
		Ask in Jesus's name	John 14:12-14
		Believe you have received	Matthew 6:6, Matthew 21:21-22, Mark 11:24, John 15:7
		Pray for people to spread the gospel	Matthew 9:37-38, Luke 10:2
		Pray for those who persecute us	Matthew 5:44, Luke 6:27-28
		Watch and pray so that we will not fall into temptation	Matthew 26:41
		Do not babble when you pray	Matthew 6:7-8

Kingdom Fundamental	Kingdom Practice	Kingdom Behaviour	Commands & Bible References
Follow Jesus			
		Respond to the call to follow	Matthew 4:19, Matthew 9:9, Mark 1:17, Mark 2:14, Luke 5:27, John 1:43, John 21:19, John 21:22
		Don't make excuses	Matthew 8:18-22, Luke 9:57-62
		Know Jesus's voice	John 10:27-29
		Follow and serve Jesus	John 12:26
		Calculate the cost (deny yourself and take up your cross)	Matthew 10:38-39, Matthew 16:24-25, Mark 8:34-35, Luke 9:23-24, Luke 14:25-33
		Receive rest from Jesus	Matthew 11:28-30

Kingdom Fundamental	Kingdom Practice	Kingdom Behaviour	Commands & Bible References
Follow Jesus	Submit to Jesus's lordship		
		Choose the narrow way that leads to life	Matthew 7:13-14, Luke 13:24-30, John 14:6
		Receive the kingdom of God like a child	Mark 10:15, Luke 18:17
		Believe in Jesus	John 14:1, John 5:24, John 6:29
		Repent of our sins	Matthew 4:17, Mark 1:14-15, Luke 13:3, Luke 13:5
		Be born again	John 3:7
		Take Jesus's yoke and learn from him	Matthew 11:29-30
		Seek first the kingdom of God	Matthew 6:33, Luke 12:27-31
		Come to Jesus	John 7:37-39

Kingdom Fundamental	Kingdom Practice	Kingdom Behaviour	Commands & Bible References
Follow Jesus	Pursue holiness (integrity / purity)		
		Live with integrity	Be perfect - Matthew 5:48 Pursue righteousness - Matthew 5:20 Pursue purity of thought - Mark 7:20-23
		Address our own issues and faults before challenging others	Luke 6:41-42, Matthew 7:3-5
		Do not cause others to stumble	Matthew 18:6-7, Mark 9:42, Luke 17:1-2
		Do not take oaths (watch what you say)	Matthew 5:33-37
		Store up treasures in heaven	Matthew 6:19-21, Luke 12:33-34
		Let our light shine before others	Matthew 5:16
		Rejoice, including when being persecuted	Matthew 5:11-12, Luke 6:22-23, Luke 10:20

Kingdom Fundamental	Kingdom Practice	Kingdom Behaviour	Commands & Bible References
Follow Jesus	Live out Kingdom values		
		Live honourably	Honour God's law - Matthew 5:17-19, Matthew 19:18-19, Mark 10:19, Luke 18:20
			Honour our parents - Matthew 15:4
			Do not covet (guard against greed) - Luke 12:15
			Honour marriage - Matthew 19:6, Matthew 19:9
			Do not commit adultery - Matthew 5:27-28
		Practise giving, praying and fasting	Matthew 1:1-18
		Practise justice, mercy and faithfulness	Matthew 23:23
		Give to God what is God's and to authorities and others what is due to them	Matthew 22:19-21, Mark 12:17, Luke 20:25
		Trust in God's provision and peace	Matthew 6:25-26, John 14:27, John 16:33
		Celebrate the Lord's Supper	Matthew 26:26-27, Luke 22:17-20
		Be ready for Jesus's return/ keep watch	Matthew 24:42-44, Matthew 25:13, Mark 13:32-37, Luke 12:35-40, Luke 17:22-25, Luke 21:8-9, Revelation 22:12-14

Kingdom Fundamental	Kingdom Practice	Kingdom Behaviour	Commands & Bible References
Follow Jesus	Exercise discernment		
		Guard against falsehood	Beware of false teaching - Matthew 16:6, Matthew 16:11-12 Beware of false prophets - Matthew 7:15-20
		Do not be deceived	Matthew 24:23-28, Matthew 24:4-5, Mark 13:5-9 and Mark 13:20-23
		Be wise as serpents and innocent as doves	Matthew 10:16
		Do not throw our pearls to pigs	Matthew 7:6
		Do not blaspheme against the Holy Spirit	Mark 3:29-30, Luke 12:10

Kingdom Fundamental	Kingdom Practice	Kingdom Behaviour	Commands & Bible References
Love your neighbour as yourself			Mark 12:31, Matthew 22:39
		Love one another	John 13:34-35
		Love your enemies	Luke 6:35, Luke 6:27-29, Matthew 5:44
	Make disciples		
		Go, make, and baptise disciples	Matthew 28:19, Mark 16:15-20
		Teach disciples to obey Jesus	Matthew 28:20
		Feed Jesus's sheep	John 21:15-17
		Preach to all nations and then the end will come	Matthew 24:14, Mark 13:10
		Testify of Jesus to others	John 15:26-27

Kingdom Fundamental	Kingdom Practice	Kingdom Behaviour	Commands & Bible References
Love your neighbour as yourself	Forgive (don't judge) others		
		Do not judge others	Matthew 7:1-2, Luke 6:37
		Do not despise little ones	Matthew 18:10
		Forgive without limit others who offend us	Matthew 6:14-15, Matthew 18:21-22, Mark 11:25, Luke 17:3-4
		Be gracious	Do not be angry with other disciples - Matthew 5:22 Be reconciled to those who have offended us - Matthew 5:23-25, Luke 12:58-59
		Correct other disciples (Christians)	Matthew 18:15-17

Kingdom Fundamental	Kingdom Practice	Kingdom Behaviour	Commands & Bible References
Love your neighbour as yourself	Undertake acts of service / generosity		
		Lead by being a servant of others	Matthew 20:26-28, Mark 9:35, Mark 10:44-45, Luke 14:10-11, Luke 22:24-26
		Wash the feet of others	John 13:14
		Do unto others as we would have them do unto us	Matthew 7:12, Luke 6:31
		Do more than is expected from us even when this is difficult	Matthew 5:38-41
		Provide for those who cannot repay us	Luke 14:12-14
		Give generously for the benefit of others and we will be rewarded	Matthew 5:42, Luke 6:30, Luke 6:38

Teach Them to Obey – Studies For Disciples

ISBN Paper Version: 978-1-9164405-1-7.

ISBN eBook Version: 978-1-9164405-4-8.

An in-depth consideration of the themes of Jesus's teaching. The content comprises fourteen thought-provoking sessions on the commands of Jesus for those who want to become more intentional disciples.

The studies address each of the twelve themes set out in this *All That I Have Commanded You* book with two additional studies that provide an important start and conclusion to considering these themes.

The first study recognises the Essential Need for the Holy Spirit in our Lives rather than attempting to obey Jesus in our own strength.

Studies 2 to 4 centre around the Kingdom Fundamental to Love God and its two supporting Kingdom Practices.

Studies 5 to 9 concentrate on the Kingdom Fundamental to Follow Jesus and four related Kingdom Practices about our personal attitudes, actions, and behaviours.

Studies 10 to 13 examine the Kingdom Fundamental to Love Your Neighbour as Yourself and three Kingdom Practices that explain how we are to do this.

Lastly Study 14 looks at the Outcomes from Putting Jesus's Command into Practice.

These studies are for followers of Jesus who want to become (and teach others to be) more intentional in their walk with Jesus, living out their Christian life biblically and practically in a chaotic twenty-first century world.

Each study within this *Studies for Disciples* book presents:

- An "Introduction" section that reinforces where we are in the overall structure (fully presented in Figure 20 in this *All That I Have Commanded You* book) as well as a study-specific diagram.

- A "Biblical Support" section consisting of a subset of scriptures that underpin relevant elements of the Kingdom Fundamental or Kingdom Practice principles and their supporting Kingdom Behaviours. This subset has been drawn from the material presented in Chapters 2 to 4 above.

- An "Our Context" section that provides perspectives on those scriptures so readers can better understand how they might apply to us today.

- A "Kingdom Fundamental/Kingdom Practice Application" section that includes thoughts on Jesus as our example, outlining where scriptures reveal Jesus effectively practising the Kingdom Fundamental or Practice under discussion, as well personal reflections on the relevant Kingdom Fundamental, Practice, and Behaviours.

- A "Kingdom Fundamental/Kingdom Practice Health Check". This includes questions and issues for individuals, couples, and group study participants to consider, discuss, and reflect upon, together with ideas for moving forward in their personal walk of faith.

- A "Possible Action" element for recording anything readers may feel the Holy Spirit is prompting them about as a result of working through the material.

- Lastly a "Memorising the Structure" section that provides an opportunity for readers to test whether they understand the arrangement of the emerging themes of Kingdom Fundamentals and Kingdom Practices.

Throughout the book, a number of diagrams, in a small range of layouts, have been included that help to build and demonstrate the simple structure that is the focus of the material. Some readers may find these particularly useful, whilst others may prefer to concentrate more upon the text.

If you are wanting to be more intentional in your life as a follower of Jesus, this might just be the book to consider.

www.ingramcontent.com/pod-product-compliance
Lightning Source LLC
Chambersburg PA
CBHW071408080526
44587CB00017B/3217